# My Body

# My Body

# Emily Ratajkowski

METROPOLITAN BOOKS

HENRY HOLT AND COMPANY   NEW YORK

Metropolitan Books
Henry Holt and Company
*Publishers since 1866*
120 Broadway
New York, New York 10271
www.henryholt.com

Metropolitan Books® and m® are registered trademarks of
Macmillan Publishing Group, LLC.

Library of Congress Cataloging-in-Publication data is available.

ISBN: 978-1-250-81786-0

Our books may be purchased in bulk for promotional, educational,
or business use. Please contact your local bookseller or the Macmillan
Corporate and Premium Sales Department at (800) 221-7945, extension
5442, or by e-mail at MacmillanSpecialMarkets@macmillan.com.

The names of some individuals have been changed to respect
their privacy.

First Edition 2021

Designed by Kelly S. Too

Printed in the United States of America

1  3  5  7  9  10  8  6  4  2

To Sly

You painted a naked woman because you enjoyed looking at her, you put a mirror in her hand and you called the painting *Vanity*, thus morally condemning the woman whose nakedness you had depicted for your own pleasure.

The real function of the mirror was otherwise. It was to make the woman connive in treating herself as, first and foremost, a sight.

—John Berger, *Ways of Seeing*

# CONTENTS

# My Body

My Body

# Introduction

WHEN IT WAS released in the summer of 2020, Megan Thee Stallion and Cardi B's viral single and music video "WAP" (an acronym for "Wet-Ass Pussy") exploded, receiving 25.5 million views within twenty-four hours and debuting at number one on the US and global charts, becoming the first female collaboration ever to do so. Soon after, the internet was consumed with a debate about the hypersexual aspects of the lyrics and video. Many cultural commentators praised the song as a sex-positive anthem and claimed that, in rapping about explicit sexual details and their desires, Cardi and Megan were asserting their agency and enacting an overdue role reversal. Others argued that the song and video were setting feminism back a hundred years.

The last time a music video sparked such a heated

debate around women's empowerment and sexuality was in 2013, with "Blurred Lines," cowritten and performed by Robin Thicke, Pharrell, and T.I. The video featured three women dancing around almost completely naked. I was one of those women.

"Blurred Lines" propelled me to overnight fame at age twenty-one. To date, the censored version, which partially conceals our nakedness, received approximately 721 million views on YouTube and the song is one of the best-selling singles of all time. The "uncensored" version was removed from YouTube soon after its release, citing violations of the site's terms of service; it was restored and then taken down again, only adding to its controversial allure.

I and, more specifically, the politics of my body were suddenly being discussed and dissected across the globe by feminist thinkers and teenage boys alike. Critics condemned the video as "eye-poppingly misogynistic" because of the way my fellow models and I were objectified.

When the press asked me for my position on the video, I surprised the world by answering that I didn't feel it was anti-feminist at all. I told reporters that I thought women would or at least should find my performance empowering. My statements about "Blurred Lines" came in the era of the feminist blogosphere, of *Lean In* and headlines such as "Why Women Still Can't Have It All" on the cover of major magazines but before the popular embrace of the term *feminist*, before Beyoncé danced in front of a giant neon FEMINIST sign, and before fast fashion companies began selling FEMINIST T-shirts. Many were outraged that the naked girl from the viral music video had dared to call herself a feminist, while others, mostly younger women, found my perspective refreshing. I argued that I felt confident in my body and my nakedness, and who was anyone to tell me that I wasn't empowered by dancing around naked? In fact, wasn't it anti-woman to try to tell me what to do with my body? Feminism is all about choice, I reminded the world, so stop trying to control me.

A few years after "Blurred Lines," I wrote an essay entitled "Baby Woman" about growing up and the shaming I'd experienced around my sexuality and developing body. Even as a working model and actress, I claimed that I hadn't experienced the sense of humiliation I'd felt when my middle school teacher snapped my bra strap to scold me for letting it slip out from beneath my tank top. To me, girls sexualizing themselves wasn't the issue, as feminists and anti-feminists would have us believe, but shaming them was. Why were we the ones being asked to adjust? To cover up and apologize for our bodies? I was tired of feeling guilty for the way I presented myself.

My perspective was the result of an adolescence filled with mixed signals related to my developing body and sexuality. At thirteen, I'd been confused when my father quietly suggested that I "not dress like that, just for tonight" when my parents and I were getting ready to go out to a nice restaurant. I looked down at the pink, lacy top and push-up bra I wore. My mother always told me to take pleasure in the way I looked, and this particular ensemble brought me validating attention from both adult men on the street and my peers at school. Suddenly, I felt embarrassed by the very thing that was also a source of pride.

I hadn't understood the time when my cousin, who was nearly twenty years my senior, came rushing into her living room, breathless, after leaving me alone with her male friend for a few minutes. I didn't understand what she was afraid of, although I already instinctively knew what her friend's body language meant—the way he reclined back on the couch, his hips jutting forward and his mouth forming a crooked, inviting smile. I was a child, but somehow already an expert in detecting male desire, even if I didn't completely understand what to make of it: Was it a good thing? Something to be afraid of? Something to be ashamed of? It seemed to be all these things at once.

I end "Baby Woman" with an exchange I had with a drawing teacher after my first year of art school. As I showed him a charcoal nude of mine, he suggested, "Why not draw a woman with a waist so small she falls over and cannot stand up?" He advised me either to "play into the stereotypes of the beauty standard or to show its oppression." I didn't want to believe that it was so stark, that those were my only two options.

For most of my life, I thought of myself as savvy, a hustler. I understood that I had a commodifiable asset, something the world valued, and I was proud to have built a life and career off my body. All women are objectified and sexualized to some degree, I figured, so I might as well do it on my own terms. I thought that there was power in my ability to choose to do so.

Today I read that essay and look at interviews from that period of my life and feel a tenderness toward my younger self. My defensiveness and defiance are palpable to me now. What I wrote and preached then reflected what I believed at the time, but it missed a much more complicated picture.

In many ways, I have been undeniably rewarded by capitalizing on my sexuality. I became internationally recognizable, amassed an audience of millions, and have made more money through endorsements and fashion campaigns than my parents (an English professor and a painting teacher) ever dreamed of earning in their lifetimes. I built a platform by sharing images of myself and my body online, making my body and subsequently my name recognizable, which, at least in part, gave me the ability to publish this book.

But in other, less overt ways, I've felt objectified and limited by my position in the world as a so-called sex symbol. I've capitalized on my body within the confines of a cis-hetero, capitalist, patriarchal world, one in which beauty and sex appeal are valued solely through the satisfaction of the male gaze. Whatever influence and status I've gained were only granted to me because I appealed to men. My position brought me in close proximity to wealth and power and brought me some autonomy, but it hasn't resulted in true empowerment. That's something I've gained only now, having written these essays and given voice to what I've thought and experienced.

This book is full of the ideas and realities that I was unwilling to face, or perhaps incapable of facing, earlier in life. I had made a practice of dismissing experiences that were painful or incongruent with what I wanted to believe: that I was the living testament of a woman empowered through commodifying her image and body.

Facing the more nuanced reality of my position was a difficult awakening—brutal and shattering to an identity and a narrative I'd desperately clung to. I was forced to face some ugly truths about what I understood as important, what I thought love was, what I believed made me special, and to confront the reality of my relationship with my body.

I'm still grappling with how I feel about sexuality and empowerment. The purpose of this book is not to arrive at answers, but to honestly explore ideas I can't help but return to. I aim to examine the various mirrors in which I've seen myself: men's eyes, other women I've compared myself to, and the countless images that have been taken of me. These essays chronicle the deeply personal experiences and subsequent awakening that defined my twenties and transformed my beliefs and politics.

# Beauty Lessons

## 1.

"When you were born," my mother begins, "the doctor held you up and said, 'Look at the size of her! She's beautiful!' And you were." She smiles. I've heard this story many times.

"The next day he brought his children to the hospital just to see you. You were such a beautiful baby." This is where the recital normally ends, but this time my mother is not done. A familiar innocent expression spreads across her face before she continues, one that I'm used to seeing right before she says something to me or my father that she knows she maybe shouldn't. I brace myself.

"It's funny," she says with a small smile. "My brother was talking to me recently . . ." She starts to imitate him and his East Coast accent. "'Kathy, Emily was a beautiful baby. But not as beautiful as you were. You were the most beautiful baby I've ever seen.'" She shrugs and then shakes her head as if to say, *Isn't that wild?* I wonder briefly how she expects me to respond, until I realize she is staring out the window, no longer paying attention to me.

## 2.

I am in hair and makeup on a photoshoot, making conversation with the hairdresser's assistant. "Is your mother beautiful? Do you look like her?" he asks, running his fingers through my hair.

He sprays product on my ends and studies my reflection in the mirror in front of us. He compliments me on my eyebrows. "They're good," he proclaims, grabbing a brush.

"What's your ethnicity, girl?" This conversation is one I'm used to having on set; it almost always goes exactly like this, and I want to shut it down as quickly as possible. I don't like the way white women use the question as an opportunity to list their ethnicities in an attempt to sound quote unquote exotic: *I'm thirteen percent this and seven percent that.* Instead I tell him simply: "I'm a white girl." My hairdresser laughs.

"Okay, white girl." He grins broadly. "I can tell you got something in there, though." He purses his lips and shifts his weight, popping a hip. He is mostly Mexican, he tells me.

"What about your mama?" He repeats his question, genuinely curious. "Is she beautiful like you?"

"Yeah," I say. "She's prettier than me." My hairdresser's eyebrows shoot up. He goes back to brushing the extension he's holding. "Well, I'm sure *that's* not true," he offers. I'm used to people sometimes getting uncomfortable when I say this.

"It is true," I respond matter-of-factly. I mean it.

### 3.

My mother is classically beautiful: she has wide-set green eyes, a tiny, elegant nose, a small frame, and, as she would say, an hourglass figure. Throughout her life she has been likened to Elizabeth Taylor, a comparison I agree with. People of a certain generation used to tell her that she looked like a young Vivien Leigh. Both *National Velvet* and *Gone with the Wind* were films my parents owned and kept in a small VHS collection next to their bed. As a child I watched these films countless times, feeling as if I was getting a glimpse of a younger version of my mother, immersed in a world of Southern belles. Vivien Leigh would bring her chin down to side-eye Clark Gable and I'd think of my mother's tales of adoring boys standing on the lawn below her bedroom window in high school. I'd imagine the silky texture of her homecoming-queen sash and the weight of the sparkling crown she wore in her yearbook pictures.

## 4.

There is a wooden bureau in my parents' living room that holds their silverware and china. Framed pictures, souvenirs from their travels, and a few of my father's smaller sculptural works sit on top of it. Guests are always drawn to one of the frames, containing two circular images playfully angled toward each other. On the right is a black-and-white elementary school picture of my mother, her hair in short pigtails. On the left is a photo of me at around the same age, a black headband sweeping my hair away from my face. Two little girls smiling widely. If it weren't for the texture of the old photograph and the year printed in the bottom right-hand corner of my mother's picture, one might think these images are of the same child. "Who is who?" guests ask.

## 5.

My fine hair always had a tendency to tangle. When I was a child, my mother used a detangler spray and a comb after bathtime to brush out the knots. The tugging stung my scalp, and my neck would ache from holding my head up for her. I hated the process. I'd fix on the bottle of detangler covered in pictures of sea animals and stare at the smiling orange seahorse and chubby blue whale as tears streamed down my face. The smell of the sweet spray made my mouth water. Feeling her comb dig into my scalp, I'd yell out in misery, "Don't!"

The house I grew up in didn't have ceilings, only stunted walls that stopped short of the roof, so my cries would fill the entire space. Hearing my howling, my father would start singing from the other room, "Hair wars, nothing but hair wars," to the tune of the *Star Wars* theme song.

## 6.

I was not raised in any religion, and talk of God was not a part of my childhood. I've never prayed much, but I do remember that as a young girl I prayed for beauty. I'd lie in bed, squeeze my eyes shut, and concentrate so hard I broke out in a sweat underneath the covers. I believed that for God to take you seriously, you had to make your mind as blank as possible and then focus on the expanding spots of light behind your eyelids and think only of the one thing you desperately wished for.

"I want to be the most beautiful," I'd repeat over and over again in my head, my heart in my throat. Eventually, when I could no longer resist the other thoughts drifting into my mind, I'd fall asleep, hoping that God would be impressed enough by my meditation to answer my prayer.

## 7.

My mother's father, Ely, was a stern and serious man. He was born in 1912 and came through Ellis Island from a small shtetl in what was then Poland and is now Belarus. A talented pianist, he graduated from Juilliard at the age of fifteen and went on to become a chemist and to father three daughters and a son. He told my mother that it was inappropriate for her to just say thank you when people told her she was beautiful. He didn't feel she had accomplished anything.

"What have you done?" he would ask. "Nothing. You've done nothing."

## 8.

I knew from a young age that I hadn't done anything to earn my beauty, just as my grandfather had pointed out to my mother. Was it, then, that my beauty was a thing my mother had given to me? I sensed at times that she felt entitled to it in some way, like a piece of bequeathed jewelry, one that was once hers, one that she'd lived with her entire life. It had been passed down to me heavy with all the tragedies and victories she had experienced with it.

## 9.

"Wear whatever you want, Ems," my mother would always tell me. "Don't worry about other people." She wanted me to be free of shame, to be able to embrace the way I looked and whatever opportunities it presented.

At thirteen, I was sent home from a formal dance because the chaperones deemed my dress too sexy. My mother had bought it with me. It was baby blue and made of a stretchy lace material that clung to my newly developed breasts and hips. When I came out of the dressing room, unsure of myself, she stood up and hugged me.

"You look absolutely lovely," she said, smiling warmly.

"It's not too sexy?" I asked.

"Not at all. You have a beautiful figure." My mother never wanted me to think that my body or my beauty was too much. "If people have an issue with it, that's their problem," she'd say.

When she picked me up from the dance, I was in tears, humiliated and confused. She tucked my hair behind my ear and wrapped her arms around me. Those people could go fuck themselves, she said. She made a special dinner and let me watch a dumb movie while I ate. Later, with my permission, she wrote a fierce letter of complaint.

"I'll read them the riot act," she declared.

## 10.

I tried to gauge where my parents thought I belonged in the world of beauties. It seemed important to them both, especially to my mother, that their daughter be perceived as beautiful; they enjoyed telling friends about the way people approached me to model and, later, about my modeling successes once I signed with an agency in middle school. They thought of modeling as an opportunity they should pursue as responsible parents. "She can make a lot of money. Does she have headshots?" a woman once asked in the checkout line of our local grocery store. When we returned to my mother's car in the strip mall's parking lot, I burst into tears. "I don't want headshots, Mama!" I'd understood the word to mean needles in the head.

Eventually, my parents found me an agent and began driving me to shoots and castings in Los Angeles the way my classmates' parents drove them to local soccer tournaments. My father put my first modeling "comp" card (an index-sized card with my dimensions and modeling images, typically left with clients at castings) on the wall by his desk in the classroom where he taught. When I was in high school, my mother framed a 9½-by-11-inch black-and-white image of me from a photoshoot and placed it on the kitchen counter facing the front door, so that anyone coming in was immediately greeted by my pouty lips, bare legs, and teased hair.

I was embarrassed by the picture and its location. After I'd moved out of the house, I convinced my mother to remove it. By that point, it had been there for several years. "You're right," she said. "It doesn't represent you anymore. You're more beautiful than that now."

### 11.

Beauty was a way for me to be special. When I was special, I felt my parents' love for me the most.

### 12.

The first casting my mother took me to was for a denim company that made expensive jeans I'd never owned. She called in a sub to teach her class so that she could drive me to Los Angeles, and I left school early, hopping into her VW Bug in the middle school's parking lot to make the commute.

She sped on the freeway, her sunglasses on. "I asked your agent about your chances on this audition. She thought I meant your chances of 'making it'! She said, 'She definitely has a shot but it's always tough to say.'" She glanced at the rearview mirror, her two hands on the steering wheel. "I meant your chances for this casting! Not for fame." She shook her head. "I didn't like that at all." They were getting ahead of themselves, she explained.

Inside the casting office, we were met with a blast of cool air and floor-to-ceiling glass doors. White benches lined the room and screens hung on the wall indicating the rooms assigned to various auditions. I walked a few paces in front of my mother, wearing the inexpensive, stretchy version of the denim company's classic jeans and chunky black boots, both newly purchased from Ross Dress 4 Less. In my heels I stood almost a foot taller than her.

We settled down on a bench and I felt my feet in my unfamiliar boots, the way the zippers cut into the inside of my foot. A freckled boy with wild, naturally highlighted curly hair sat a few feet away from us.

"Emily?" A young woman held a clipboard to her face and then scanned the benches. I stood up.

"Flip your hair," my mother whispered. I swung my head forward and felt the blood rush into my face, my hair surrounding me. I came back up, my hair falling to either side of my face. I could feel my mother's eyes on the back of my head as I disappeared into the casting room.

On the car ride home, I rested my head in my hand and stared out the window. The sun hit my cheek as the freeway flew by.

"That boy looked at you when you stood up and flipped your hair," my mother said. "He was watching you."

*What did he see?* I wondered.

## 13.

My mother liked to recount stories about men noticing me from the time I was twelve ("I'll never forget the look on his face as you walked past him! He stopped dead in his tracks and his mouth fell open!"). But she also believed that men's understanding of beauty was limited and unrefined.

"Marilyn Monroe was never really *beautiful*," she'd say to me, when my father would make an approving face at mention of her.

She made distinctions; there were women whom men found appealing and then there were true beauties. "I don't *get* Jennifer Lopez," she'd say, wrinkling her nose. "I guess men like her." I learned over time that "men liked her" ranked far below "beautiful" but was decidedly preferable to not being mentioned at all. She could be quite condescending when speaking about such women: "She's cute," she'd say, smiling sweetly, a subtle trace of pity in her tone. When we'd watch a film featuring a young female actor, my mother would almost always remark on her looks: "I mean, she's not a *beauty*." She also did this with my friends, casually assessing their appearance as we shopped. "She's certainly not pretty, but she does have a nice figure," she'd proclaim as she inspected California avocados for their ripeness.

## 14.

After I left home, my parents made a habit of posting professional pictures of me on their Facebook pages. My mother responded to each comment from her friends with a "Thank you so much, Suzy!" or "We are so proud of her, Karen." My father responded to his friends, too, but instead of saying thank you, he liked to joke: "She has my heart and soul and that's about it, Dan." I read his comment and thought of the time he told me that I'd inherited his nose.

"It's kind of big," he'd said, laughing. My mother scowled. "Don't say that, John," she whispered, her voice low and disapproving.

## 15.

My mother seems to hold the way my beauty is affirmed by the world like a mirror, reflecting back to her a measure of her own worth.

She says, "A friend of mine from college wrote on Facebook that he'd seen your recent magazine cover. He said, 'No surprise Kathleen's daughter is beautiful! But she's not as gorgeous as you, Kathy. No one compares to you.'"

My mother loves to remind me of the time she'd been complaining about the way some women had treated her, and I, at the age of three, declared, "They're just *jealous*, Mama!"

She recites this story as a charming testimonial to my sweet and perceptive nature at a young age. It wasn't until I was older that it struck me: How had I already been introduced to the concept of competition between women before I had even learned to read? How had I understood so early that my remark would provide my mother some solace for the unkindness she experienced?

## 16.

I find other ways of constructing a mirror not unlike my mother's. I study red-carpet and paparazzi images of myself online and in the camera roll on my phone, tapping the screen to zoom in on my face as I try to discern whether I am actually beautiful. I scroll Reddit, reading and weighing the comments in my thread, wondering if I am "overrated," as one user notes, or in fact "one of the most beautiful women in the world," as another says. I learn from one commentator who claims to have worked on the crew of a recent shoot of mine that I am "nothing special in person," and from a different user that, after seeing me at a coffee shop around the corner from my apartment with my dog, she can say that I am "way prettier IRL. Better than in her pictures."

I post Instagram photos that I think of as testaments to my beauty and then obsessively check the likes to see if the internet agrees. I collect this data more than

I want to admit, trying to measure my allure as objectively and brutally as possible. I want to calculate my beauty to protect myself, to understand exactly how much power and lovability I have.

## 17.

I was lying in bed after sex with my first serious high school boyfriend when he began to tell me about the other girls he'd slept with. He described their bodies, their hair, what he liked about them, and I listened, feeling a sudden sense of panic. My stomach twisted. I began to sweat. *What is wrong with me?* I wondered. *Why was my body responding this way to my boyfriend talking about other girls he'd found attractive?*

As he went on, all the muscles in my lower abdomen and glutes clenched, and I knew that it was a matter of minutes before I'd have to run to the bathroom. He kept speaking, unaware of the way I'd curled into myself underneath the thin comforter. I started to shiver. He continued. "She . . . Her . . ." I nodded and asked questions, feigning indifference, knowing that I would later spend hours looking these girls up, watching them at school, collecting data on how we were the same and how we were different. I finally got up and rushed to the bathroom, scared that I would not be able to hold it in any longer. Although I knew that these girls from my boyfriend's past, or his mention of them, was not an actual threat to my safety, my body reacted as if it was. I hated that he might ever have found anyone more attractive than me.

## 18.

Some of my mother's memories are so visceral to me that I sometimes can't remember if they are her experiences or my own—like the one where she went to the women's restroom at a party in the early days of my parents' courtship (as she would say). When my mother came out of the stall, my father's ex-girlfriend was at the sink, washing her hands in front of a wide mirror. My mother stood next to her. "And I thought, well, there we are. So different. You know?" There they were: the two women of my father's choosing. I imagine them, perfectly still, their arms loose at their sides and their faces blank. Maybe one of the faucets is still running. My mother is nearly a foot shorter than the blond woman my father once lived with. The pale skin of her broad shoulders and long torso shimmers. Her hair smells like salt water. My mother's dark, curly hair frames her heart-shaped face, and the curves of her hips are silhouetted against the white tile of the bathroom. Both their faces are in shadow as they assess themselves and each other.

## 19.

My mother liked to tell me that she'd always wished for hair like mine.

"Like a sheet of satin," she said, eyeing me while slipping her hand over the top of my head as I squirmed away.

"Don't, Mom!" I snapped, instantly hating the sound of my voice as it pierced the air.

"I know, I know," she sing-songed, "Now you're a teenager who doesn't want to be touched, but you'll always be my baby."

"I wanted hair like yours my whole life," she said again, quietly, suddenly more serious. "I would iron my hair on an ironing board to make it straight like Jane Asher's." She stared off into nothing, contemplating an alternate life, a world in which the only difference was the texture of the hair on her head. (*But what a difference that would be!* I could imagine her saying.)

Now I realize I wasn't being a typical teenager. I just didn't want to be looked at by my mother, because I knew that when she watched me she was often calculating: examining and comparing.

## 20.

As a young woman, I hated receiving compliments on my appearance, whether they came from my girlfriends or the men and boys I was interested in. A guy I dated briefly in my early twenties used to make fun of me for how awkward and uncomfortable I'd become when he'd tell me he thought I was beautiful. "Oh my God! You can't handle it!" he'd say, watching me as I instantly grew self-conscious.

"Shut up." I'd roll my eyes, trying to indicate that he was wrong.

"But you're a model, you're like, known for your beauty," he'd say, confused, waiting for an explanation. I never knew how to answer. I wanted to tell him that I didn't need boys I liked to say that. I was happy to hear that kind of thing on set, when I was making money, but in my private life, I didn't want it. Some part of me was attempting to resist the way I'd learned to conflate beauty with specialness and with love. *No thanks*, I'd think. *I don't want whatever it is they're trying to offer. I don't want their mirror. I don't want that "You're the most beautiful" kind of love.*

### 21.

My mother stopped coloring her hair in her early sixties, letting it go gray, then silver, and then, finally, white. She continued to wear it short, its natural volume giving her head shape. She looked pretty, an adjective rarely used for women over sixty, but accurate for my mother and her elegant features, made softer with age.

"Getting old is strange," she told me one morning, sitting on my blue couch by the window in my Los Angeles loft. "I was walking down the street the other day and saw two attractive young men approaching. I didn't even think about it, but I stood up a little straighter to walk past them." She let out a small laugh. "And they didn't even look at me. And right then I realized that I'm invisible to them now. All they see is just a lady with gray hair!"

She looked lovely in the natural light as she spoke.

"I guess it's just the way it goes." She shrugged. There was a peacefulness to her. I imagined what it would be like to one day no longer be noticed by men.

"Perhaps it's somehow freeing?" I asked.

"Maybe," she said finally.


## 22.

I am newly married to my husband when he remarks casually, "There are so many beautiful women in the world."

I freeze when he says this. I know it is a perfectly acceptable and truthful thing to remark on, and yet I feel a familiar twist in my gut.

"What?" he asks. He can feel the switch; he can sense the instant tension in my body.

"I don't know," I reply. I press my face into his chest, ashamed of my reaction. "I don't know why it hurts to hear you say that."

I can tell he wants to console me, but he is confused. I want him to console me, too, but I am unsure why I need it. Why do I suddenly feel as if he doesn't love me enough?

## 23.

In the small, windowless room that is my therapist's office, I tell her about my reaction to my husband's remark. I explain the gut pain. The assessing. The other women.

"Apples and oranges," my therapist tells me. "What if you're not the same as other women, what if you're an entirely different fruit?" she asks gently.

I hate that I am having this conversation; a part of me is horribly embarrassed. I want to stand up and scream, *Of course I know this! I hate women who compare themselves to other women! I am not that way!*

But there is a version of myself who needs to hear what she is saying because there is also a part of me that wants to correct her. "But everyone has a favorite fruit," I tell her. I feel a tear run down my cheek. "Everyone prefers one over the other. That is how the world works; everything is ranked. One is always better than the other."

# Blurred Lines

WHEN I DROPPED out of college to work full-time as a model, I liked to tell friends that the French word for *model* is *mannequin*.

"So," I'd say, shrugging, "I'm a mannequin for a living."

Around that same time, I caught a terrible stomach flu and lost ten pounds in one week. After I recovered, I kept the weight off, realizing that I was booking more shoots with my thinner body. I began wearing platform shoes at all times (even when I dressed in the dark to arrive at a shoot before sunrise) because I never wanted to give clients the opportunity to see that I was shorter than most models. I became skilled with time management, something I'd constantly struggled with in high school and in my only year of college, when I was perpetually the girl walking into class ten minutes late. I learned the traffic patterns of Los Angeles, making sure to always wake up with time to spare, and alerting my agent if I was even just a few minutes behind. I let clients photograph and style me however they wanted even when I hated the way they made me look. I made these adjustments to my behavior and attitude and body with one objective in mind: money.

I considered my life and work as a model as a temporary situation, one that protected me from the fate most of my older friends had suffered after the financial crash in 2008, when they had to move back into their parents' homes, saddled with student debt, and return to the service industry jobs they'd held as teenagers.

Money meant freedom and control, and all I had to do to fund my independence was learn to become someone else a few times a week: strip down and get greased up in body oil to pose suggestively in red lace lingerie or brightly printed bikinis I'd never choose to wear, pouting at the command of some middle-aged male photographer.

Once I quit school—and got the flu—I reached a new level of financial success. Lingerie and swim shoots paid more than the normal day rate for a standard e-commerce job, and I had several clients who booked me regularly for what my body did for their products. I remember coming out of a dressing room in a lingerie set and one female client remarking that it was "hard to find girls that are so skinny and can also fill out a bra." My cup size was a valuable and rare asset, one that translated directly to higher paying jobs. It also limited the type of work I could do, though; I was a "commercial swim" girl, meaning that I could shoot catalogs but I'd never work in high fashion.

The more money I made from modeling, the more I enjoyed having it. I had no rich friends, and for that reason I kept my indulgences private, driving alone to a clothing store where, only a year or so before, my high school girlfriends and I had never dared to buy anything, only occasionally stopping by to look. We'd leave quickly the moment a salesperson asked, "Can I help you girls with anything?" Now I luxuriated in going into the store alone, gripping my faux leather purse and touching the hanging garments with the tips of my fingers, feeling a thrill go up my spine as I responded, "Yes, thank you, I'd like to try this on." Sometimes I'd buy an item of clothing and other times I'd leave empty-handed, elated by the experience either way. One night, after a solo shopping excursion, I wore a brand-new navy jacket to meet a friend. She asked me when I'd bought it.

"Today," I told her. She shook her head.

"Damn," she said. "So nice to just be able to walk into a store and pick something out whenever you feel like it, huh?" I studied her, relieved to see that she

wasn't resentful. I felt embarrassed by the new difference in our lives but also grateful she could appreciate
my pleasure. She was right—it *was* so nice.

I found a cheap ground-floor loft to lease in Downtown Los Angeles and paid $1,250 a month in cash,
dropping off a thick envelope with my landlord, who
stank of patchouli oil and lived in the loft directly
above me. The space was entirely concrete and had
only one window, complete with metal bars, which
looked out on a parking lot. The ceilings were so low
that in the platforms I'd come to wear religiously I
could reach up and place the palms of my hands flat
against them. None of this bothered me, though; I was
thrilled to have what I considered to be a spacious loft,
many times bigger than any place I'd lived in previ-
ously. I painted the walls and ceiling white and pinned
dollar-store Christmas lights around the headboard of
my bed.

One of my favorite things to do after a day of work
was to pick up some Thai food from a takeout place
close to my building and sit on my bed, complete with
the quilt I'd bought from Urban Outfitters for sixty
bucks and the bed frame I'd borrowed from my parents' house. Nights like these were what I lived for; I
couldn't imagine anything more luxurious or enjoyable.

I liked to explain to people that I paid only a dollar
per square foot when they asked why I lived so far
from Hollywood, the center of the modeling industry. I took pride in being in what was called the Arts

District, a neighborhood that was considered funky and up-and-coming. It was quite a commute, at least a forty-five-minute drive to most of my shoots and castings. But I liked the distance the loft offered me from the world of photographers, agencies, and clients, and most of all I liked the identity my edgy neighborhood bestowed on me. On my drive home from work, I'd transform back from mannequin to myself.

Within a year, I was featured in a few editorials for a Los Angeles–based magazine that got the attention of several blogs and fashion and men's sites, leading my agent to suggest a trip to New York to meet with agencies on the East Coast as well as *Sports Illustrated* and Victoria's Secret.

"But aren't I too short for New York?" I asked.

The same agent had told me only a year or so before that the fashion world was not an option for me. "There's just no point in you trying to be something you aren't," she'd said simply.

"Not necessarily," she told me now, avoiding my eyes. As the number on my scale went down, the number on my checks had been going up. The agency had taken notice.

I stayed in a tiny hotel room in Midtown with rough beige carpeting and a small instant-coffee maker that I used each morning before my castings. There was no proper full-sized mirror in the room, so I climbed onto the bed in my heels to check my outfit before grabbing my portfolio and heading out. Despite the expense, I took taxis to castings, reading the addresses from my email, not confident enough to navigate New York City's subway system. Still, I was mindful of how much money I was spending, knowing that the cost of the flights and hotel would be deducted from my next paycheck.

I felt tiny as I entered the grand lobby of the Victoria's Secret building. A man in a crisp suit and tie greeted me from behind a long silver desk.

"Casting?" he asked, his eyes heavy and his expression blank. I nodded, encouraged that he had identified me as a model. *Maybe I do belong here*, I thought.

Upstairs, I waited alone below a silver Victoria's Secret sign, surrounded by giant blown-up black-and-white images of recognizable models—or, as Victoria's Secret referred to them, "angels"—arching their backs and holding index fingers up to their mouths as if flirtatiously telling me to shush. A floor-to-ceiling screen displayed a parade of long-legged women strutting down a runway, wearing sparkling lingerie and large, colorful wings. They came toward me, one after another, their hair bouncing as they smiled wide, their eyes looking just beyond mine. They were the goddesses of this large, modern office building and these screens were their shrines. They were mannequins, too, I knew, but they seemed to feel powerful in a way I never did. I wanted to be one of them. I sat mesmerized until a woman came out from behind two double doors and greeted me, pulling my attention away.

"Follow me," she instructed, glancing at my platforms and then quickly at my face. I stayed a few paces behind her as she led me through an expansive open-plan office. No one looked up from their desk as we passed. She opened a door to a small room filled with drawers of bras and underwear and directed me to take off my clothes in the corner.

"Shoes, too, please," she said, pointing toward my feet. I walked on my tiptoes over to a wall where she silently measured my height and took several flash images of me with a digital camera, making a note on a piece of paper before thanking me, barely glancing up as I scurried out the door.

Afterward, I headed uptown to meet with an agency.

"We don't love the shorts," they told me, inspecting the pair of black denim cutoffs I was wearing over tights. "Can you take them off?"

I nodded. "Of course," I responded, slipping the frayed cutoffs down my legs and over my platform boots.

"Much better," said a young woman with a French accent as she studied my hips. "Now we can see how small you are! We'll be in touch."

The next day, I made sure to leave the shorts at home, dressing only in a black crop top and tights. I stood on the bed, checking the small mirror to make sure that the tights weren't too sheer.

At my *Sports Illustrated* casting, two female editors leafed through the heavy plastic pages of my portfolio.

They glanced from the pictures back to me and asked if I ever smiled. "We like girls who smile here at *SI*!" they explained, shutting my book with a thud.

Back on Seventh Avenue, I huddled over my iPhone, desperate to return to my hotel room and crawl beneath its unfamiliar sheets. I stood in the sun, enjoying the break in scrutiny, when a man approached me, staring at my crotch. "I can see your pussy," he muttered without meeting my eyes. I felt the sting of shame but refused to let myself cry.

Through the years, I'd developed a necessary and protective immunity to the frequent disappointments and rejections that came with modeling. I didn't allow myself to become excited about shoots or potential jobs; I didn't care if my image ended up on a billboard or in a magazine as long as the check cleared. I wasn't interested in fame or notoriety, just the cash, or at least that's what I told myself. In New York, I broke my own rules: I let myself imagine the power, beyond money, that other women seemed to have gained by becoming successful. I returned to Los Angeles with a renewed sense of resolve and determination. Fine, I wasn't going to be a supermodel, but I was going to make as much money as I possibly could with the options I had.

It was around this time that an email came in through my agent about a music video featuring T.I. and Pharrell, whom I admired, and a singer called Robin Thicke, whom I'd never heard of. Attached to my agent's email was a treatment, a PDF filled with words and pictures describing the director's vision for the video. Lying in bed that morning, I scrolled through the document: Bright red text spelling out "#THICKE" paired with images shot by Terry Richardson of topless, red-lipsticked girls with messy hair were interspersed with bolded phrases like "Let's break the fucking rules!" A section entitled "TONE" listed "TRUE PIMP SWAG, DUMB SHIT IN A VERY SMART CONTEMPORARY WAY, VICE MAG STYLE" and "NAKED GIRLS XXX TITS BUSH RED LIPSTICK." I read the misspelled text underneath the section "THE GIRLS" out loud to the guy I was seeing at the time:

"SHE'S THE BEST KIND OF GIRL, SHE'S 100% CONFIDENT. THIS IS FAR FROM MASOGYNIST. IT'S GIVING CRAZY PROPS TO GIRLS TO HAVE THIS UNBELIEVABLE SENSUAL VISUAL POWER."

I was surprised to see that the director was a woman. I searched the email for the rate. "Oh, wow," I said. The fee was barely more than I got for shooting one day of e-commerce for Forever 21. "Fuck that. Basically just another shitty music video with a bunch of naked girls." I told my agent to pass that same morning.

But Diane Martel, the director, persisted, sending me a personal note: Could I at least come and meet her to discuss the project? The list of music videos Diane had directed—Beyoncé, Mariah Carey, JLo—was certainly impressive. When my agent said he thought there was "room on the money," I agreed to drive to West Hollywood, struggling to parallel park in a metered spot in front of a photo studio on Santa Monica Boulevard.

Inside, Diane remained seated as I stood in front of her wearing a minidress and heels, gripping my portfolio, which she did not ask to see. She told me that the director of photography would be a young woman I'd worked with recently called Olivia. I softened at the mention of her name. I'd liked the pictures she'd taken of me; they were pretty and ethereal, and there had only been women on set when we worked together. "I've known Olivia her whole life," Diane said. "She's so talented. And so young! You know how pretty she makes everyone—not slutty. And it'll be mostly all women behind this." Her leg bounced rhythmically as she spoke. "I want this to be funny. Like a spoof. I know you're an actress. I want you to be acting in this."

"Okay," I said. "But the money still has to come up." She nodded.

In traffic on my drive home on the 10 freeway, I heard from my agent that the rate had increased a decent amount with an added bonus for overtime. I hung up and rolled down the window, feeling the air from passing cars. I figured, *What the hell. Who watches music videos anymore anyway?*

The shoot for the video was at a large studio in Silver Lake, only a fifteen-minute drive from my loft. I arrived with an empty stomach, having made sure not to eat too much the night before because I knew I'd be naked—topless at the very minimum—on set the next day. I poured myself some coffee from the craft services table and looked around. Diane hadn't lied. I was glad to see she had filled the set with women: the DP, the stylist, the props designer, and the makeup artist.

The two other models who were taking part arrived and sat in chairs next to me facing a long mirror: a striking, soft-spoken Black woman with a French accent who introduced herself as Jesse, and a blonde named Elle, who caught my eye in the mirror. A makeup artist's assistant applied red lipstick to her mouth as she put up a hand to gesture hello.

"Do you feel comfortable?" the costume designer asked as I tried on various different white undergarments and plastic see-through tops and shorts. She explained that these looks were for the censored version of the video, which we would shoot at the same time as the unrated, naked one. I liked her immediately: she had bleached hair cut into a pixie and wore Doc Martens and was the kind of girl I'd want to be friends with but hardly ever met on jobs. Diane came to the makeup room to check in with me before we began. "Do you feel good?" she asked. I ran my hands over the white underwear and nodded. I felt like I was a part of the team.

I went to the set to shoot first, leaving Elle and Jesse in the hair and makeup area. A woman only a few years older than me, wearing a white jumpsuit, introduced herself as the props manager.

She pointed toward a long table filled with various objects that were to be used in the video. "What do you want to start with?" I picked out an oversized Styrofoam hand with red nails. She handed it to me proudly; she had made it herself.

"Do you know we have farm animals coming later?"

This wasn't something I was used to: cool women around my age being enthusiastic about the job we were working on. My mood shifted. Maybe this day would be fun.

The song, which I had never heard before, began blaring across the giant soundstage. Three beats thudded in the air before a voice called out, "Everybody get up!" Olivia smiled at me from behind the camera. "Just have a good time, dance how you want!" Diane yelled through a megaphone from the dark beyond the brightly lit, pristinely white stage. I danced ridiculously, loosely, the way I would to entertain my girlfriends. I was surprised to find I was enjoying myself. Diane cracked up through her megaphone.

Robin Thicke arrived later. I was posing on all fours in underwear, a red toy car in the arch of my back. He kept his sunglasses on and waved to me and the crew, flashing a smile as he walked toward the makeup room.

Hours passed. Jesse and Elle joined me onstage

along with Pharrell, Robin, and T.I. We all barely spoke, aside from some quick introductions made by Diane, the musicians giving us a nod. They were the talent, we were more like props. I wasn't bothered; I was there to work. The animals showed up and I held a lamb in my lap, observing. Robin focused his attention on Pharrell and T.I., his teeth showing as he threw his head back in laughter, his eyes still covered by dark sunglasses. They smiled politely but did not return his animated enthusiasm.

Under the lights, our plastic shorts and tops fogged up with heat and sweat from our bodies. The smell of alcohol leaked from Robin's body as he alternated between lip synching and actual singing. The song started up for what seemed like the millionth time that day—the same three beats filled the room in hard succession. Diane continued to yell directions through her megaphone. We stripped down to our flesh-colored thongs for the unrated version. Pharrell and Elle smirked flirtatiously at each other. I put on ludicrously tall white platform sneakers and danced in front of the rest of the cast.

"Let's get these ladies a drink," Robin said to one of his assistants, and within minutes someone brought us red plastic cups half filled with ice and alcohol. I took a few sips, but I'd never particularly liked vodka and I was too hot and worn out from shooting to drink any more. The song started up again.

"Hey, hey, hey!"

Jesse looked over at me and shook her head. "Too hot," she mouthed, running a hand over her slicked-back hair. I continued to wiggle around the stage, trying to recapture the fun I'd been having entertaining Olivia and Diane. I rolled my eyes at the antics of the famous men we were working with.

The whole world saw me roll my eyes in the final, viral edit. In a matter of months, "Blurred Lines" catapulted me to global fame. The first time someone stopped me, yelling "Emily?" I was on the phone with my mother, crossing the street in my neighborhood. I looked at the man, confused, studying his face in an effort to try and place it. "I love 'Blurred Lines!'" he exclaimed, smiling widely, before asking for a selfie. I was stunned.

Online people debated whether the video was misogynistic. The way my fellow models and I were writhing—and almost naked, in the unrated version—in front of the male musicians raised eyebrows. Journalist after journalist asked me the same question: "What do you say to those who have deemed the video anti-feminist?"

The world was shocked to hear me respond that I didn't see it that way. I was secure in my body and my nakedness on set, I'd tell them honestly. I focused on how I felt during the majority of the shoot, remembering being in the company of many women I trusted and liked.

After the success of the video, I moved to New York and signed with the same agency that had rejected me only a year before. I shot *Sports Illustrated*. I was happy to discover that fame had granted me access to two new sources of income: appearances, where I could show up to an event or speak with a media outlet about a product, and sponsored posts on my Instagram, both of which paid more than what I had made in a week as a working model prior to the video.

Mainly, though, I was disoriented. I grew tired of talking about the music video and sharing my thoughts on it, feeling a distinct twinge of dislike whenever Robin Thicke's name was mentioned or placed next to mine. I was grateful for my career, but I resented that every profile began with a mention of "Blurred Lines," a music video I'd only agreed to do in order to make some money. I didn't know how to marry the identity and ego that I'd kept as separate as possible from my work with the one that the world was now labeling a sex symbol. Since I'd been in high school, modeling had just been a job, and now suddenly it seemed to be who I was. I flailed. Continuing to relate to my work passively, I signed up to be in movies that I didn't have any interest in and modeled for brands I thought were lame.

I floated through the next couple of years. In between frequent shoots and travel, I spent too much time on the internet and in bed and out drinking with people I didn't particularly like. I knew that by most standards I should be happy—I'd achieved the thing that all aspiring actresses and models are thought to want:

to be known for their beauty and desirability. "You've made it!" the friend who had commented on my navy jacket years before wrote to me on Facebook, reminding me of how the world viewed my "success."

But I wasn't just *famous*; I was famously sexy, which, in many ways, felt gratifying. It had seemed obvious to me that the most desirable, attractive woman was always the most powerful in any given room, just like the Victoria's Secret models who marched toward me on that giant screen. And in many ways, my life did change. Strangers greeted me with enthusiasm. Famous men I'd had crushes on as a child hit on me. Beautiful women talked to me as if I were one of them. I was on the covers of magazines, got invited to glamorous parties I'd never dreamed of attending. Forget Thai food and chain-store quilts—now I was being sent endless boxes of free designer clothes. I could show up at popular restaurants in New York or Los Angeles and be seated whenever I liked. And I had more money than I'd ever imagined making: I put a down payment on a loft only a few blocks from my place in the Arts District, this time a place with a giant window and plenty of light and a pool on the roof. I was even able to give my parents some cash.

Yet I felt like I was spinning and out of control. I hadn't chosen this life, and I was unsure of how I'd ended up living it and what it meant about who I would become. I hated going to auditions, especially for TV and film, where I almost always read in front of several men who I was convinced thought very little of me. *They already think I suck,* I'd tell myself. *I'm nothing more than an LA piece of ass to them. I'm not talented. I'm not even that pretty.* I'd barely rehearse for these auditions, reading the pages once or twice before going in, paralyzed by self-loathing. Did I even want to be an actress? I couldn't remember when or how this had become the thing I was supposed to pursue and excel in. I'd always imagined myself as someone who had ideas and made decisions. I'd get in my car after one of these readings, feeling worthless, and think about how I'd rather be in the position of the men in these rooms, choosing whom to hire for *my* projects.

It was years later, when I was scrolling through Instagram half distracted, my thumb moving busily over the screen, that a photo of Robin Thicke and his much younger girlfriend appeared in my feed. I recognized her face and long, lean body, realizing that I'd met her years before in LA when we were both working models, shooting swim and lingerie e-commerce in shitty warehouses in Alhambra and Vernon. She'd just had a baby, *E! News* announced. I looked through her photos, studying the wideness of her smile next to the bloated softness of her partner's jawline. "I love you baby daddy!" one caption read.

I clicked on Thicke's handle, surprised to see my screen fill with white. "User Not Found" and "No Posts Yet" were placed next to his name. I'd been blocked. I racked my brain to figure out why. Had I said something in the press that might have offended him? Then I remembered something that had happened on the "Blurred Lines" set that I'd never told anyone about, something I hadn't allowed myself to acknowledge until that moment, half a decade later: *He did something he wasn't supposed to do.*

It was later that day, when Thicke returned to the set, a little drunk, to shoot just with me. I could tell that his mood from earlier had shifted—he didn't seem to be enjoying himself in the same way. He didn't like the lack of attention he was getting from the people hired to make *his* music video.

Now it was just him and me, alone on the tundra soundstage. He was dressed in a black suit and I was in nothing but white sneakers and a flesh-colored thong. The same three notes; same Diane yelling through her megaphone; same sweat dripping; same "Everybody get up!"

Again I danced as ridiculously as possible. Diane yelled excitedly, "You're fucking funny! Make that face again!" Robin put his sunglasses on as he sang along, his vague annoyance palpable.

Suddenly, out of nowhere, I felt the coolness and foreignness of a stranger's hands cupping my bare breasts from behind. I instinctively moved away, looking back at Robin Thicke. He smiled a goofy grin and stumbled backward, his eyes concealed behind his sunglasses. My head turned to the darkness beyond the set. Diane's voice cracked as she yelled out to me, "Are you okay?"

I nodded, and I may have even smiled, embarrassed and desperate to minimize the situation. I tried to shake off the shock. I walked away from the set and the warm lights, crossing my arms over my bare chest. I felt naked for the first time that day. The music stopped. I stood by the monitor for a moment and glanced around at my new friends. No one, not one of us, said anything.

Diane finally spoke. "Okay, well, no touching." She addressed no one in particular, her megaphone now hanging loosely at her hip. I pushed my chin forward and shrugged, avoiding eye contact, feeling the heat of humiliation pump through my body.

I didn't react—not really, not like I should have. Neither did any of the other women. Despite how many of us were there and how safe I'd felt in their presence, we were in no position to hold Robin Thicke accountable on the set of his music video. We were working for him, after all. We paused awkwardly, and then we continued shooting.

When journalists asked me about the video over the years, I didn't allow myself to think of Robin Thicke's hands on my breasts, or of the embarrassment I'd felt standing naked in front of Diane. I was defensive—protective of the environment she had tried to create on set and of the other young women who seemed like they could've been my friends. I was also ashamed—of the fun that, despite myself, I'd had dancing around naked. How powerful I felt, how in control. I wondered:

What *if* I had yelled in Robin Thicke's face and made a scene? Stopped the shoot? Maybe my big break never would've happened.

In my early twenties, it had never occurred to me that the women who gained their power from beauty were indebted to the men whose desire granted them that power in the first place. Those men were the ones in control, not the women the world fawned over. Facing the reality of the dynamics at play would have meant admitting how limited my power really was—how limited any woman's power is when she survives and even succeeds in the world as a thing to be looked at.

With that one gesture, Robin Thicke had reminded everyone on set that we women weren't actually in charge. I didn't have any real power as the naked girl dancing around in his music video. I was nothing more than the hired mannequin.

# My Son, Sun

I WAS FOURTEEN the first time Owen forced himself on me. We were lying on the crusty carpet of his mother's condominium. It was early morning, and I was so exhausted that I could barely keep my eyes open. I wanted water, but there was none. I remember the way his skinny jeans tightened over his erection, and I remember the dirty shoelace he used as a belt. I'd told my parents I was sleeping over at a friend's house so I could stay out all night and go to house parties. Owen, who was sixteen, had said that's what I should do. He'd positioned himself as my guide to a new school and a new world. I believed he was my way into meeting new people. It was only later that I realized he didn't have many friends himself. My status as a hot freshman girl was what got him the invite to those house parties in the first place.

I remember his freckled skin and pale stomach and how his nose started bleeding when he was on top of me. "It's the Accutane," he said, blood dripping onto my collarbone. His blood was so red it looked fake, as if it came from a bottle of ketchup. The texture was as thick as syrup. He wasn't embarrassed. I remember the way that red looked against his bright blue eyes. I remember his long blond eyelashes as they blinked, elegant and in slow motion as he held his hands to his nose.

When Owen got my number and texted me to hang out over the weekend initially, I'd lied to him.

"My mom's family is in town, so I'll be spending time with them. Sorry!" I reread the text silently before I hit send. *A perfectly reasonable excuse*, I thought, closing the screen and hoping he'd go away.

"Ha ha," he responded immediately. "Who hangs out with their family all weekend? We can go out after ur done with them. There will b a cool party on Saturday we can go to. I'll drive." I was embarrassed. How could I be such a child as to think that hanging out with family was a valid excuse to miss parties? I was in high school now; I needed to act like it. Besides, I didn't want to be with my parents on the weekends anyway.

"Okay," I wrote back. I didn't know how to say no.

I never felt safe with Owen and always wanted to go home when I was with him. But I suppose home didn't feel right either. This, *he*, seemed like the real world. This was high school, this was being an adult: scary and out of control just the way everyone said it would be. I wanted to rise to the occasion, prove I was ready to handle it.

One night, Owen drove to an empty parking lot and started to kiss me. I thought I had to kiss him back since he'd taken me to a few parties, so I let him fumble in my pants with his hand. I wish someone had explained to me that I owed him nothing. I wish someone had instructed me not to get into his red truck at all. I wish that when the cops pulled up, I'd told them that a part of me was relieved to see them. I wish they hadn't said I was on the wrong path, that I could end up doing drugs, that I was bad, and had instead said, "We're worried about you; you're still a kid. Let us take you home; this isn't your fault."

I wish that a couple of years later when, breathless and sobbing, I'd revealed to my mom that I wasn't a virgin, she'd hugged me instead of looking disappointed. I didn't give her the details—Owen, the carpet, the blood—I only said that I'd had sex. We were in her car, pulled over a few blocks from her sister's house. I was in the passenger seat, still not old enough to drive. The fabric of the seat was hot against my back. "We wondered, but we were sure: not Emily," she said, her eyes fixed on the windshield. I could see her already thinking about how she'd share this news with my father. I winced. She exhaled. "We're late to see my family."

Her tongue clicked against the roof of her mouth. She started the car back up.

I took deep breaths and slowly managed to calm down. I tasted my snot and bit my upper lip. I felt gutted, as if my insides had been hollowed out. My body was light and fragile, like a shell doomed to shatter, as I walked through my aunt's front door, a bell jingling as it swung open. I greeted my extended family, feeling my uncle's cool skin against my cheek when I hugged him, knowing that they'd be even more disapproving of me than my mother had been. I felt bad for her; sorry to have confessed something about myself that was so shameful she now had to hide it. I wanted to curl up and fall asleep forever, but instead I sat in the shadows of my aunt's yard and pretended to smile.

Owen came over to my parents' house once, unexpectedly. I remember how animated and sloppy he seemed as I opened our front door and he stepped into the living room. An air of drama surrounded him. His skin was red and his eyes glassy.

"My dad and I were fighting," he announced, gasping, his face contorting.

I was awkward as we sat on a wooden bench on the back deck. Owen laid his head in my lap, and thick tears streamed down his nose. I looked at his profile, his large features and the red pockmarks on his face. Everything about him seemed fresh and raw, like a wound that had just broken open. His eyelids were practically translucent. I shifted uncomfortably beneath the weight of his head. I wasn't sure what to do with my hands.

I could sense my mother's eyes on us, watching through the glass of her bedroom door. The house was quiet. My parents stayed inside and out of sight. It seemed as if everyone understood the role I was supposed to play. I inhaled and drew up a memory of how I thought a woman behaved when she comforted a man. Maybe it was a moment from a movie? I wasn't sure. My mother had told me about her high school boyfriend Jim, that he came from an unhappy home and had often slept on her family's couch. What did she do when Jim came over? I tried to embody that version of my mother, her love for Jim. I pushed away my tangle of confusion and slowly, very slowly, touched the curls in Owen's hair.

"It's okay," I said tentatively. "I'm so sorry, Owen," I whispered with more confidence; the warmth of his hot face radiated against my thighs. It felt good to do what was expected of me, but something about my comforting of him wasn't right. I had been cast as the loving and concerned girlfriend, but I didn't want the part.

After Owen left, my mother said to me, "I'll never forget what you looked like, his big head in your lap." She'd witnessed something theatrical. "Poor Owen," she added.

When I started hanging out with Sadie and the other popular girls, they scoffed if Owen approached us. "He's kind of gross, Emily," they'd say. I didn't like the way they looked at him, but it also felt good to have someone say I shouldn't be with him; their disapproval gave me permission to avoid him. I began to feel more confident about ignoring his texts and less afraid of abandoning him.

After I finally broke up with Owen—or rather, after I escaped him—I was riddled with guilt. Food was unappetizing. I couldn't sleep, knowing Owen might show up at my parents' house or hurt himself to spite me, which he had threatened to do. My phone buzzed late into the night with text after text. He was relentless. He'd sit in his dad's blue VW Bug across the street from my house, just in sight of the window of my living room. The blue stood out unnaturally against the foliage of the street; it was the same color as his eyes, both milky and crisp at once.

By the time I was fifteen, Owen had stopped parking across the street. One night, I made plans to go drinking with a group of girls who weren't really my friends. I'd never spent time with them outside of school. They were cooler than me, or at least it felt that way. They all lived in big tract houses with walk-in closets and parents who never seemed to be home. We got ready for the night at one of these houses, in a pink room with a full-length mirror, watching ourselves and each other as we tried on outfits. One girl used a Sharpie on our arms to tally the shots of vodka we were knocking back. I remember tripping over a pile of clothes and looking down at the black lines that started at my elbow and traveled down to my wrist.

The next thing I knew, we were in a dark parking lot next to a car that smelled like leather. A grocery store's sign glowed in the distance. My mouth was slick and my stomach felt tight and I could not stop throwing up. I could not hold myself up. The girls exchanged looks, annoyed, as they held my hair back from my face. The boy who was driving us must have called Owen, because suddenly his truck was there and he was pulling me off the asphalt and dragging me away. I'd not spoken to him in months. I squeezed the arm of one of the girls and tried to conjure the words to tell her he was not safe, but she'd already turned away. He'd come to claim me, and they thought of me as his.

I woke up with Owen on top of me. I was in a small bed in a blue room. I tried to use my arms to push against his chest, to force him off and away, but I was too weak and too drunk. My vision flickered with ghostly white shapes and blue light. My mouth felt like cotton and I could taste the smell of his skin. I wanted it to be over but I didn't know what to do, so I shut my eyes tightly and made small noises, the noises I thought women were supposed to make during sex.

Why did my fifteen-year-old self not scream at the top of her lungs? Why did I whimper and moan softly instead? Who had taught me not to scream?

I hated myself.

The next morning, I walked up my parents' driveway in clothes that were not mine, and mumbled two or three words about being tired. I got in the bath and made the water as hot as possible, but I couldn't stop shivering. I lay there for a long time, watching my skin turn red from the heat. I was barely able to move; every limb felt impossibly heavy and my whole body ached. It was a bright day and the light in the bathroom was yellow; the walls seemed high and I felt tiny. The blond hairs on my arms stood up straight against the faded black Sharpie lines.

I slept deeply that night. When I woke, I found I was a new and different version of myself. I dressed carefully, ate plain toast, and sat quietly next to my father as he drove me to school. I looked ahead out of the window, my seatbelt on, hands delicately placed in my lap. I didn't tell anyone what had happened that weekend with Owen. This is what you do. This is the beginning of how you forget.

What felt like a lifetime later but was closer to a year, Owen texted me again. He was no longer at my school, and I had a new boyfriend and a different set of friends. He wrote long paragraphs, manic blocks of texts that arrived on my phone with a whoosh. He told me he'd been in and out of rehab for heroin, that he'd lost twenty pounds, and that a girl from another high school had accused him of raping her at a party. "Things have been really bad," he said. "I shouldn't be alive." I didn't respond. I was afraid that if I replied, he would somehow draw me back into his life.

Someone else filled in the details of the rape accusation for me. The girl had been very drunk at a house party. She'd ended up in a bedroom, away from the rest of the party, barely conscious. Owen had come into the room and taken advantage of her. She and her family were pressing charges.

When I first heard this, I couldn't stop thinking about the girl Owen had hurt. I pictured her home. I pictured her father. I imagined her hair and her room. I could see her saying confidently, "I didn't want that," without shame, without blaming herself. Why hadn't I developed that skill? I longed to be more like her. I wanted to be able to say, *I didn't want him*, to myself and to my friends and to the whole damn world.

I told my mother about the girl, what she said Owen did, her parents. "Well . . ." She trailed off. She seemed displeased, as if I'd brought up something that wasn't polite or appropriate. I could tell she didn't know what to say. I remember feeling gruff and tougher than her. I lived in the Wild West, a place where terrible, unspeakable things happened every day, and she was a lady. It felt like my responsibility to protect her from those types of horrors. I didn't let myself be disappointed that she hadn't said more. It was better this way, better that she couldn't offer insight or comfort. The less I needed from her, the less opportunity she had to let me down.

I did eventually tell a girlfriend about Owen. We were high, and I was lying on her soft mattress and gazing at the string of lights she'd woven into her bed frame. I told her about him and his red truck and the black lines on my arm. My friend was sitting cross-legged on the edge of her bed. She had a lip piercing, and I remember watching her bite it while she stared at me, listening. "That sounds like rape, Emily." My head snapped over to her.

"What? No," I said quickly. I blinked and turned back to the ceiling, feeling dizzy. I knew she was right.

\* \* \*

I was nineteen, in an airport in the Midwest, waiting for a connecting flight back to California after a quick catalog shoot, when I learned that Owen was gone forever. At that point, I was used to flying by myself and navigating airports—used to sitting on cold linoleum floors and falling asleep in uncomfortable chairs and moving through crowds of people. I was sitting cross-legged, charging my phone in an outlet low to the ground, scrolling through Facebook on my iPhone when I saw the update. An older boy from high school had written his name and "RIP." My first thought was that he'd misspelled Owen's last name. *He'd be so sad to see that*, I thought. *But of course they'd misspelled his name; he'd never had any real friends.* My chest tightened.

"What happened? Is this real?" I texted a few old

acquaintances to see if they had any information. Some part of me already knew the answer.

It wasn't until I was jammed into my middle seat and the flight was beginning to ascend that I finally got a response.

"It's real. He passed away." I read the words as the pressure of the cabin pushed me down into my seat. The plane lifted into the air. My ears rang.

He was gone: his flesh, his eyes. He was no longer pulsing with blood and life. He was no longer anywhere. I would never have to see him again.

"Are you all right?" a woman in the aisle seat next to me asked quietly. The roar of the plane nearly drowned out her voice.

"I'm sorry," I said. "I just found out that the first guy . . . the first boyfriend I ever had . . . he's dead." I felt my tongue swell. She laced her brows together.

"I'm so sorry." She sounded so genuine that I wondered for a second if she'd ever known this feeling, this mix of loss and relief over the death of someone who'd hurt her. I wondered how to articulate it, to her, to anyone. I put the tray table down and rested my face in my hands.

Owen had died of a heroin overdose, alone, at twenty-one. His body was locked in the guesthouse he'd been renting, locked in there for three days before anyone figured out where he was. The police had to break down the door.

I attended the funeral alone, and chose to stand at the back of the crowd. We were on a cliff above the ocean. The sky was endless blue. I squinted my eyes to watch Owen's father speak. He said that when the police brought Owen's body out from the guesthouse, he'd sobbed. His beautiful baby boy was dead. He'd said, "My son, feel the sun," as the California sun beat down on Owen's pale, lifeless body.

"My son, sun, son," he wailed.

*   *   *

A few weeks after I'd told Owen I didn't want to see him anymore, he'd driven us to a college forty-five minutes out of town, paying for gas with crumpled and filthy dollar bills he'd made by working construction. "Just let me take you to this concert," he'd texted me. He'd gotten the tickets months before, and I still wanted to go. I wanted to prove to myself that I was in control, that I wasn't vulnerable to his manipulations. "Okay. But we're going as friends," I clarified.

"As friends," he agreed.

I made sure to wear new clothes that he'd never seen before, and white boots I'd picked up at a thrift store that made me feel older and self-assured. I acted distant and unbothered when he picked me up. This was the kind of thing adult women did: hang out with guys they'd once been intimate with but no longer were.

He stood behind me, not touching me, as we watched

the concert. The lights lowered as the band began to
sing a quiet ballad:

> *Love of mine, someday you will die . . .*
> *If there's no one beside you when your soul embarks*
> *Then I'll follow you into the dark*

Sitting on the plane, I felt the memory of Owen standing behind me; tears rolled down my face. I cried, but
not because I wouldn't see him again. I cried because
I couldn't believe I was the type of person who'd gone
to that concert with him, who'd unwillingly lost my
virginity to him. I cried because, unlike the girl who'd
accused him of rape, I hadn't been able to say, *I was
violated.* I cried because I felt guilty for abandoning
Owen. I cried because I hadn't left him earlier. I cried
because I was sure that I was someone who did not
deserve to be safe. I cried for the loss of a different
life, one that was full of experiences and people of my
choosing. I cried because I didn't feel like the heroine
of my own life. I cried because I was ashamed of being
so incapable of control.

"Please, never come find me," I whispered into my
palms underneath the hum of the plane. "I don't want
to be in the dark with you."

And then, firmly: "Owen, no."

# Toxic

I WAS SIXTEEN on February 16, 2007, when pictures of Britney Spears shaving her head hit the internet. At the time, I was smoking pot every day after school, having regular—and unprotected—sex with an older boyfriend who never once brought me to orgasm, and working as a model, driving myself up to LA from San Diego a couple of times a month and skipping class for photo shoots. That was the year I posed for a surfing magazine as their "Taste of the Month." I was tanned and topless in the picture, wearing only a black bikini bottom, turned away from the camera, my bare back making the shape of an S. I coyly looked over my shoulder, my mouth open, a little surprise in my eyes. I was a junior in high school.

No one could've missed the image of Britney leaning

toward the mirror, wild-eyed and smeared with mascara, delicately holding a clipper in her hand, intently shaving her head. She is smiling in the photo, elated, like she just heard a good joke and is enjoying it. Strands of long brown hair still cling to the crown of her head, a reminder that Britney had once been here.

That same year I helped Sadie, a girl I knew from school, sign with my modeling agency. She had more of a fashion model's body than I ever did; she stood 5' 9" and weighed no more than 110 pounds, whereas I was considered short and curvy (a "swim girl," my agents told me when they took my measurements). All her life, Sadie had heard that she had the right physique for fashion, even when she was just a kid, surfing and dreaming of being an athlete. She had Amazonian legs, built to run and kick, as if ready for battle. She parted her jet-black hair on the side, securing it with a simple barrette and scooping it into a precise ponytail that sat at the nape of her neck. In profile, she was mostly cheekbone, with a wide button nose and pillowy red lips. Her swan neck looked as if it could easily twist all the way around or dip toward the ground like a Slinky.

Even when she wore white lacy baby-doll dresses and delicate droplet earrings, Sadie seemed dangerous, like she was built of weapons she had yet to master.


SADIE LIVED TEN minutes away from our high school, in a gated community off the 101, and was mostly friends with boys, specifically one cool, older group. They called themselves the Scab Crew, drawing the letters *SC* all over their skateboards. She'd get stoned with them at lunch; from the windows of my third-period Spanish class, I'd watch her stride back to campus, late. She'd swing open the heavy door of our room, mutter, "Sorry," half-heartedly, and plunk herself down in a plastic chair in the back. Our eyes would meet and she'd grin as she unwrapped the foil around a giant burrito, which she'd proceed to eat loudly, cementing her bad-girl reputation.

My dad was the painting teacher at our high school. The Academy was the alternative public school in the district; it functioned on a system of quarters instead of semesters and offered classes like Skate PE. We had a surf team but no football. On gray Saturday mornings, the popular upper-class girls would wake up early and drive to various beaches to watch the surf team compete. They'd stand barefoot in the sand, wearing zip-up hoodies over their bikinis and waving their hands in the air, screaming the boys' nicknames from the shore.

I'd transferred to the Academy from middle school knowing no one but my father and a few of his fellow teachers. My dad wore flip-flops every day and wouldn't take attendance until the end of class. To have his class after lunch was "the dream"; you could come back as late as you wanted, and stoned, too. Everyone was convinced that my dad's policies were lax because he was a former hippie and pothead, but I knew that wasn't true. He simply enjoyed his reputation as a chill teacher. The cute guys on the surf team adored him, calling him Rata. "Rata is a legend," they'd say, their eyes red and their skin freckled from too much sun.

The year before I arrived, my dad told some of the surf-team boys that his daughter was coming to the school in the fall. "Keep an eye on her," he said.

On the first day of my freshman year, I put on a thin red tank dress over a push-up bra and rode to school with my dad in the cab of his Toyota pickup truck. The Academy had no dress code, and I was thrilled to be able to wear whatever I wanted. It felt new, an exhilarating adult freedom. I walked to classes, keeping my head still as upper-class boys passed by me, exclaiming loudly enough for me to hear: "Yo, that's Rata's daughter!" "She's hot, dude." I gripped my three-ring binder to my chest.

Later, word got around that "Rata's daughter models." It wasn't just the way I looked that made the boys notice me; it was also my perceived status in the outside world as an attractive girl. I was scared by the older boys' attention, but also glad: the way I looked was getting me noticed in a new school, and I was grateful not to be invisible.

Sadie was often with those boys. She had all their numbers in her phone, saved under their nicknames. She knew which classes they were taking, what plans they had for the weekend, where they lived, and which girls they thought were hot, remembering the names of the freshmen with big boobs and the sophomores with bedroom eyes. She made sure to say hi to these girls and compliment them on their outfits when she saw them in the hallway. This is how she and I started spending time together.

Within a few months, the boys began inviting me to lunch off campus. I'd awkwardly accept and meet them in the parking lot, surveying the crowd for a familiar black ponytail. We'd usually spend our thirty minutes talking about my dad. "Have you ever smoked with him?" they'd ask, peering at me from the driver's seat. (No.) The pretty, popular girls took note of who grabbed the boys' attention, watching me climb into their Nissans and Toyotas with suspicion and interest. Some chose to be mean or ignore me completely; Sadie decided to bring me closer.

On weekends, she'd drive a packed carful of boys around to their skate spots. Her boyfriend, Mike, always sat shotty. Pulling a furiously heavy U-turn, she'd screech to a stop beside me, her head sticking all the way out the window, both hands on the wheel, her long arms extended forward.

"Emski—get in!" she'd shout. I'd crawl into the cramped backseat, balancing on a guy's lap, ducking to avoid hitting my head on the car's roof as she put her foot on the gas and tore out.

Before she started modeling, Sadie had a job as a cashier at a sandwich place by the beach. I was impressed that she always had cash on hand. "From my tips," she'd say, as she pulled out a handful of dollars to pay for gas, burritos, handles of alcohol (purchased by any means: our terrible fake ID; friends who were older), spontaneous shopping trips, whatever she wanted. She was only a year older than me, but I felt as if she were an adult and I a kid.

When Sadie got drunk at house parties, she'd stand on the street in front of her parked car and play-fight with one of the Scab Crew, usually whichever guy was the most fucked-up. She'd laugh deeply and kick suddenly and expertly high in the air, her hands clenched into tight fists near her chest. She was taller than most of the guys, and at some point they'd tell her they'd had enough.

"Chill, Sadie. Seriously!"

Some of them, though, liked this opportunity to hurt her. When that happened, I'd usually move a couple steps away and nervously pretend to text. But Sadie seemed to especially enjoy the fighting when one of them got into it, grabbing her wrists and pushing against her as hard as he could. She wanted the challenge. She seemed to want to feel them try to hurt her.

Eventually the guy would succeed, and Sadie would throw herself to the ground, collapsing, legs splayed. I remember her crying then, lying on the cement, wailing. When I got on my knees to comfort her, she'd jolt up abruptly and push past me, frowning and chasing after one of the guys, never so much as glancing my way.

When we arrived at parties together, I knew that, from the outside, we made sense as friends. But when we were alone together, without anyone there to watch us, I was unsure as to what Sadie wanted from me. She seemed to know how to act in any situation, how to be cool with the right people and disregard those of no consequence. She wore the right shoes for any occasion, laughed at jokes that everyone but me understood, and shoplifted like a pro, managing to steal her prom dress from our shared department-store fitting room as I walked dutifully to the cashier to pay for mine. What could I offer her? Other than the occasional emotional drunken fit, which seemed mostly like a simple bid for attention, she appeared solid. She understood the world so much more clearly than I did. She might have been born at seventeen, long-legged and aloof, swerving around town, her car loaded with the Scab Crew. She was a natural at navigating the world of boys. I could only hope to learn from her.

* * *

"Britney went fucking crazy," Sadie whispered in the middle of our computer class, pulling up the infamous picture on her screen. This was the era of Lindsay Lohan stumbling out of clubs, white powder on her nose, underwear (or the lack of it) peeking out between stick-thin legs; of Amy Winehouse's tiny hips and bloated midriff and big hair. We were used to these images. But when Britney shaved her head it was something different, something we couldn't understand. We studied the picture and wrinkled our noses.

"She looks fucking ugly," Sadie sneered.

I felt angry; Britney was destroying the girl I'd once idolized. As an only child who'd spent an inordinate amount of time with her baby-boomer parents, I missed a lot of the socializing and pop culture that my peers experienced. I remember watching the precocious girls in my fifth-grade class dance to Christina Aguilera's "Genie in a Bottle," mesmerized and full of envy and curiosity as they swung their hips in perfect coordination, twelve-year-old girls in matching low-rise black jeans and crop tops, moving together as one organism. I didn't have a Spice Girls phase and I didn't know the words to any Backstreet Boys songs. I never saw *High School Musical* or *The Simple Life*; my parents refused to let me watch television at home.

But I did have Britney.

One Christmas, I specifically asked for Britney's debut album, *Baby One More Time*. I was fascinated by her expression in the video for the eponymous song, the way her eyes looked innocently up into the camera, her face framed by pink pom-poms and pigtails. She was at school, in uniform, and I wanted to know how Britney did it, how she looked so enticing even within the confines of school and all its rules. I played the CD for my mother, wanting to share in my excitement. It was a rainy Christmas, and the clunky CD player was perched on a windowsill. I danced in front of it and sang along. "She's good, right?" I asked.

My mother made a face, scrunching up her nose. "Not to me. I don't like it."

I rolled my eyes and kept dancing, chalking up her disdain to our different tastes and generational divide. I didn't understand that she might have an objection to songs like "Born to Make You Happy," in which a seventeen-year-old Britney sings:

> I *don't know how to live without your love,*
> I *was born to make you happy.*

Maybe my mother hadn't been aware of the lyrics, though; I don't know.

When we all learned that Britney had lost her virginity to Justin Timberlake, I was twelve and desperately wanted to ask my parents about it. I wanted to know if that was okay, or whether she had done something really bad, even unforgivable. Were they mad at her for having sex? Had she betrayed her fans, and me, specifically? What would happen to Britney now that she was no longer the same?

Even as Britney transformed and lost her innocent image, one thing remained the same: she was singular. The only women who regularly appeared around her were her backup dancers, placed strategically to draw more attention to the main attraction. Other female pop stars were competitors, neither friends or allies. Gossip magazines made visual diagrams comparing Britney to her antithesis, Christina Aguilera. When they were finally paired together at the MTV Awards, it was only to sexually swap spit with one another and Madonna. The message was clear: when women were together, it was only for the titillation of men.

A year after Britney lost her virginity, I got my first flip phone and made my ringer the instrumental version of "I'm a Slave 4 U." I knew all the lyrics by heart ("Oh baby, don't you wanna dance up on me / *Are you ready?* / Leaving behind my name and age"), and I always had Britney's face in mind when I listened to her songs: how her puppy-dog eyes would swell curiously as if we'd caught her by surprise, interrupting her and how she would stare at us, even into us, quizzically and earnestly. *What do you need?* she seemed to be asking.

\* \* \*

By middle school, I'd developed breasts and grown long skinny legs, and strangers began approaching me, often at the grocery store or the mall. They'd stride up, clutching their purses, and lean toward my mother to say, "She should *really* consider modeling." As if to say, *How could you deny your child such an opportunity?* My parents resisted at first—my mother once barked back at a woman, "She'll be a brain surgeon!"—but softened to the idea after I turned thirteen. My mother told me I could decide if I wanted to begin modeling, that it was up to me. She tells this story often, wondering, *How did this all start?*

"I'll never forget it!" she says. "You were looking out the window, we were visiting my brother in New York City, taking a cab to the Upper East Side to meet him. You turned to me and said, 'Mom, I want to try it. I'm ready.'"

This would've been around the time Britney released "Toxic," which is probably still my favorite song in her catalog. I especially like the musical interlude where she sings a long and haunting "Ahhhh, ahhhhh, ahhhh" that is cut off sharply by the sound of a DJ scratch. In the music video, Britney appears as a scantily dressed air stewardess on a plane full of old, overweight, sweaty businessmen careening through a dystopian yellow sky. Britney proceeds to spill liquid on the lap of one man, only to aggressively rub it off to the beat of the music.

*Intoxicate me now with your lovin' now*
*I think I'm ready now (I think I'm ready now)*

By thirteen, I'd learned through the hierarchy of middle school that girls who were considered hot got the most attention. They were *special*. Britney was like that—she commanded a type of power that, through modeling, suddenly seemed attainable. *I want to be one of them,* I thought.

After that visit to New York, my mother drove me

up to LA to meet with Ford Models. I wore low-rise Frankie B. jeans, my most expensive and prized item of clothing. The jeans had back pockets embellished with rhinestones, which made them hard to sit in because the hardware would pierce through the denim and into the skin of my ass. They were so low that my butt crack would peek out; I tugged up on the belt loops so often that they eventually fell off.

At Ford Models, a woman in her late thirties with curly hair measured my hips over those jeans. I looked down at the top of her head as she knelt down and circled my hips with a tape, then nervously glanced at my mother. "Thirty-four inches," she announced, folding her tape measure into her hands. Then she said more quietly, just so I could hear, "We'll take a few inches off because of these pockets."

Afterward, we sat on white chairs in the waiting room. An agent brought out a thick stack of papers covered in lines and lines of small black text. My mother signed on my behalf. "This is all happening so fast. I didn't expect this," she said as she wetted the tip of her finger to flip through the pages, her glasses on.

Apparently, when Britney arrived at the salon and told them she wanted a buzz, the hairstylist tried to talk her out of it. Britney went ahead and grabbed a clipper and started doing it herself. She said, "I don't want anyone touching me. I'm tired of everybody touching me."

* * *

After parties on the weekends, Sadie and I would crash with her boyfriend Mike, a Scab Crew guy who lived at a family member's house, a few blocks from the beach. I never laid eyes on the guy he lived with, but I knew he was fresh out of prison and had no interest in what we were getting up to. This was ideal. We could come in at any hour and be loud or stink up the house with weed. No one cared. Mike sold pot and E and coke out of his room; I don't know why he lived there and not with his parents.

Three of us would bunk in the same bed: Mike on the outside edge, Sadie in the middle, and me smooshed against the wall. I kept on whatever clothes I'd worn that night. Crunchy, tight jeans. Mini dresses. I never slept well there, but having Mike's bed to crash in meant that I didn't have to worry about a curfew.

One night, I woke in darkness, Sadie's head right next to mine on the pillow, her face turned away from me. I could make out her thick ponytail, slightly messy. Hands were reaching over her, touching me. My breasts were out of my shirt and Mike was squeezing my nipples. I froze, staring at the back of Sadie's head, as I realized what was happening. I closed my eyes and pretended to sleep, sighed, and then rolled over onto my stomach, out of Mike's reach. Goosebumps covered my torso and arms. I felt the cold air coming through the window above me and tried to breathe it in, hoping to soothe myself back to sleep.

I never told Sadie or anyone else about this late-night experience. *Had I imagined it, anyway?* I told myself that in choosing to reach over Sadie's body to touch mine, Mike had complimented me. I told myself this was the kind of thing that would make Sadie jealous, which I knew was true. *Your boyfriend likes my boobs better than yours,* I thought. Did it give me some power over her? I even started to convince myself that I liked the feel of Mike's touch. Maybe I was into it? Turned on, even? I knew that if Sadie found out, she'd blame me.

\* \* \*

That same summer, Sadie and I would stop by Ford's offices together on our weekday trips to LA when we had some extra time in between castings or needed to wait out the traffic before making the two-hour-plus commute home. Sadie would screech into the parking lot of the fancy West Hollywood high-rise and brake at the valet station with a jolt, our heads snapping forward. We'd climb out, the smell of French fries emerging with us and my legs tingling from being seated for so long. Sadie was confident in the high heels we wore on these outings, and I'd admire her gait as I stumbled behind in mine, watching the bikini string tied around her neck bounce as she moved. We both knew to always wear our bikinis underneath our outfits whenever we came by the agency.

On this particular visit, we were coming to pose for "digitals," the unretouched and "honest" pictures the agents sent to clients as references. Once we were on the twelfth floor, in an office surrounded by huge windows offering panoramic views of Sunset Boulevard and the hills above it, we stripped down to our heels and bikinis. I remember leaning over, surrounded by agents in the middle of that large, open space, pretending to adjust my heel in order to make sure my tampon string remained hidden in my bottoms.

I was allowed to buy one bathing suit each summer, and the one I wore for that afternoon had seen better days. Sadie and I had spent our entire summer at the beach, and my bright red top was fading and frayed. Booking jobs that paid meant I could get a new bikini and shiny white patent-leather high heels like the ones Sadie was wearing that day. Money meant freedom and a whole other kind of power that I was only beginning to understand but felt desperate for.

The strings of my bikini wrapped around my rib cage, pushing my boobs up and together. I arched my back and stuck my butt out as I walked dutifully behind a young assistant, past the agents sitting at their computers.

"That body," crooned a gay male agent, his eyes flashing up at me as I walked by. I grinned.

Sadie had her pictures taken after me, pushing her chin down and squinting her eyes slightly as she shifted her weight to pop a hip out. Her bikini was black and low and hit her hips just at the right point. I watched her, comparing our dimensions in my head. I felt too curvy, maybe even fat, and definitely too short next to Sadie in her heels.

"Work it, girl," the assistant said as he watched Sadie move and pose. I stood up straighter and sniffed the air, trying to see if I could smell my BO.

As soon as the digitals were done, the agent snapped, "Let's take a look at your books, girls," spinning around in his office chair, waving us over.

We shuffled over to his wide desk, still half naked, clutching our oversized white portfolios.

"Girls, you leave these in the hot car too often, I can tell. The plastic pages are wrinkling." He tsk-tsked, flipping through page after page of our pictures. "Can we get these girls some new books?" Sadie and I exchanged glances, knowing these new portfolios would show up as deductions in the fine print of our next paychecks.

I peered down as he paused at side-by-side, up-close images of my face, my lips pursed and mouth open on one page and my eyes half closed on the other.

"Now this is *the* look. This is how we know this girl gets fucked!" He pointed down at the pictures.

Sadie shoved me and smirked. "It's true," a female

agent chimed in from her desk. "We always know which girls are having sex by their pictures."

My face felt hot as I glanced from the agent to Sadie. I wanted to check in with her—was this something to be proud of?

I felt a strange sense of confidence rise up in me as the agents nodded approvingly. I was the "sexy" one, and everyone around me seemed to agree that was a good thing. It made me different and special, and maybe even powerful. I wrapped my hands around my rib cage and pushed my boobs up farther, smiling.

* * *

One of the Britney songs everyone but me loved was "Lucky." In the video Britney appears in two roles: she sings the lyrics, acting as a kind of narrator while watching over her other, more glamorous self, who receives awards and basks in the adulation of her fans. This second Britney lives in a huge, fancy, empty house and walks around alone in a pink robe and diamond necklace, staring into an old-fashioned hand mirror. At times, there are three Britneys in the frame: the narrator, the adored and lonely Britney, and the latter's reflection. Sad Britney was not what I wanted to see. I didn't want to hear about how lonely she felt despite all her success. The video ends as glamorous Britney rolls over in her bed, her makeup smeared and a look in her eye not unlike the one we'd see just a few years later, as she stared into a mirror with a clipper in her hand.

*She's so lucky, she's a star*
*But she cry, cry, cries in her lonely heart, thinking*
*If there's nothing missing in my life*
*Then why do these tears come at night?*

I don't ever recall liking modeling, really, and I've often wondered whether Sadie did either. I remember watching myself in a mirror once at a shoot, though, professionally made up, looking years older than I actually was, opening my mouth, pushing my lips out, and arching my back as the photographer clicked away. I liked my image in that moment, or at least I was struck by that girl: I was desirable; I was wanted; and I knew that if any girl from school (particularly Sadie) saw me like this, she'd be wild with jealousy. So even when I felt scared and uneasy at the apartments of middle-aged male photographers, who had me change in their tiny bathrooms, where I was surrounded by their deodorants and shaving kits and condoms, and who, as I emerged into their "studios," asked me whether I had a boyfriend or made comments about my body, I told myself I was lucky. I had photographic evidence of my value, and I was even beginning to save some money.

*Lost in an image, in a dream . . .*
*And the world is spinning, and she keeps on winning*

In high school, when I told people I was debating between college and a full-time modeling career, they'd warn me, "Models have an age limit. Their careers are over by thirty." This always annoyed me. I thought those saying it were being sexist and ageist, implying that women couldn't be older and still be beautiful. But now, I think they were right, even if by accident. Maybe women can't keep *winning* past the age of thirty.

Sadie and I drifted apart during her senior and my junior year. We'd never known how to be real friends, anyway—how to protect each other, how to talk about the things that happened to us at house parties or at castings or with agents. Early in our friendship, we began seeing one another as competitors rather than allies.

During the last summer we spent together, we hung out with a group of boys who made a habit of sneaking into a rich kid's parents' home. Mike was out of the picture by then, and we came to rely on this new place as our crash pad on late nights. We'd crawl in through a window and listen carefully, making sure no one was home. We'd push past one another to claim our rooms. Staying there felt safer than staying at Mike's ever had, even though we were undoubtedly breaking and entering.

One night I spent there with my boyfriend, I got my period in my sleep, gushing bright red blood all over the master bedroom's sheets. When we woke up, my boyfriend was convinced our cover would be blown, and that the kid's parents would have us all sent away for life because of the bloody mess I'd made of their bed. He looked at me in a panic and, embarrassed, I went and told Sadie what had happened.

Sadie followed me back into the bedroom, calmly took the sheets off the bed, and walked to the bathroom without saying a word. She pushed up her sleeves and ran cold water in the sink. I watched from behind her as the water turned brown and red. She wrung them out with her hands and then put the sheets in the washing machine. It might've been the only time I ever felt as if she was truly my friend. When I thanked her, she shrugged it off as nothing.

Eventually Sadie went off to college in San Francisco. Whenever I saw an update about her on Facebook, my stomach would tighten and twist with anxiety, remembering our time spent together and the person I was at fifteen. I stayed abreast of her life, routinely checking in on her social media every couple of months to see what she was up to. She cut her hair super short. She bleached it blond. She fell in love with a much older, punk-looking guy. She broke up with him. Her legs got skinnier, I noticed. She visited Japan. She moved to LA. She went to art school. She stopped wearing clothes that showed her legs at all.

I could feel her watching me, too. I wondered how my life appeared to her. I wished I could see it through her eyes.

One day, she wrote me a message. It was filled with over-punctuation and extended "hahaha"s, which surprised me because the Sadie I'd known had been aloof and unflappable. Now, she was over-punctuating. Too many words in all caps and extended "hahahahas."

We went back and forth, updating each other on the basics of our lives. She told me she'd run into a boyfriend of mine at a club in LA where a lot of artists hung out. *Of course she would be there,* I thought. *She is still fucking cool after all these years.* She explained that she had gone up to him and said hi.

"I was ranting about how we went to high school in a demented beach town and hung out with a lot of skaters," she said.

I bristled; I didn't want to reminisce. I was sure that somehow the conversation would lead me back to my fifteen-year-old self, silent and complicit in bed at Mike's house or uncomfortable and unsure at castings. I was embarrassed by that version of myself. I hated that Sadie had known her.

We've now lived in two of the same major cities, New York and Los Angeles, at the same time. She's an artist. We know some of the same people; our friend groups overlap. It seems that Sadie has real female friends now. Sometimes I wonder if in an alternate universe— one in which we'd become *actual* friends—we could've helped each other navigate these unfamiliar cities and worlds through our twenties. Mostly, I'm just glad to see that she has created a life that, unlike our high school existence, doesn't appear to exclusively revolve around the attention of boys and men.

I'm sorry we never focused on the right things when

they mattered most, but I'm glad to know she's okay. I only wish I'd told her in high school how strong I thought she was. How I would have liked to have known her better.

Googling "Britney shaved head" now brings up a picture I don't remember having seen. Britney's arms are raised as if she's touching what remains of her hair. There is no clipper in sight. It's almost peaceful. She's pulled back from the mirror, not looking at us but past us. Her small button nose and big doll eyes are glossy, her gaze faraway. She seems relieved. It's almost painterly, this photo, reminiscent of *Girl with a Pearl Earring*, but whereas the girl in the painting has a turban covering her head, Britney's hair is gone and in its place is her shockingly naked scalp. It surprises you. It feels violent, a warning.

# Bc Hello Halle Berry

IT STARTED RAINING on the island in the morning. We watched the drops form small, perfect circles on the surface of the pool, and S opened the sliding glass door to let in the heavy air and the sound of rain. We were silent as we lay in bed, our minds still fuzzy from sleep and our tanned bodies tucked under the crisp white sheet. My skin smelled like saltwater and expensive sunscreen, tangy and unfamiliar.

I held my coffee on my chest and stared blankly at the giant gray clouds as they inched across the sprawling Indian Ocean. Framed by the edges of the sliding door, the infinity pool bleeding into the ocean looked like a screensaver. The clouds moved so quickly that I was getting a headache trying to follow them. I felt tiny, as if I could be swept away if I wasn't careful.

Was it our third day here? Time seemed irrelevant. We were truly in the middle of nowhere, floating on an ocean on the other side of the planet. We used our thumbs to check on our lives back home, but no one was awake to deliver news anyway. It was just the two of us and our iPhones, in a room built on thick wooden stilts sunk deep into the ocean floor.

I moved slowly getting out of bed. The soles of my feet were cool against the smooth floors. The *tap tap* of the rain followed me as I walked to the bathroom. I caught glimpses of my naked body in the mirrors lining the walls. I looked freckled and young, sleepy in a way that people sometimes consider sweet and charming. I washed my face and studied myself, adding mascara to my puffy eyes while sipping my cold coffee.

*Now seems like the right time to get a photo out of the way*, I thought. S wouldn't even need to get out of bed to take the shot. I hummed to myself as I quickly ran a dry razor under my arms and squeezed lotion onto my thighs. I rummaged through my suitcase to find a bikini from my own line and began untangling a particularly stringy orange top, remembering that we'd never shot this one before. Kat, my business partner and friend, had reminded me before I left that it was important to get a picture of myself wearing this particular design. The suits generally don't sell as well if there's no photo of me in them. I pulled the bottom up and leaned over to make sure my breasts fell into the triangle top correctly.

"S," I called from the bathroom. "I need you to take a picture."

"Sure." He smiled at me as I walked, still barefoot, toward the bed. "Well, don't you look pretty," he said gently, opening the camera on his phone.

"Thanks." I felt my cheeks grow hot. When S and I first met, I'd been embarrassed by my relationship to Instagram—by the desire, at that point in my career, to increase my followers so I could continue getting paid by brands to promote their products. I hated having to ask him, as I sometimes did, to take my photo to make that happen. It took me six months to get over my shame and call upon him to participate. While cheesy, it paid the bills. The ability to make a living off my own image shouldn't be cause for embarrassment, I figured.

I moved to the center of the view, facing the water, and placed my feet on the metal ledge of the sliding glass door, just a few inches from the downpour but still dry and out of the rain. "Thought we should get this out of the way."

"Look at me," S instructed, and I did, feeling the fat of my ass fold into the back of my leg, my expression blank.

"Got it," he said, passing me the phone.

I posted the image, unfiltered, knowing that people like seeing a picture they might have taken themselves. I captioned it "Hi. This is my butt in @inamoratawoman": simple and to the point. I made sure to add tags so followers could buy the suit straight from the app.

We rode to the breakfast buffet on the bikes provided by the hotel. I put on S's tie-dye tank top over my bikini and one of the hotel's rain-resistant hoodies over that. As our sneakers pushed against the pedals, all we could hear was the soft tapping of raindrops hitting thick, oversized green leaves, and the crunch of our rubber tires against the white sand. We raided the opulent buffet, two plates each, piled high with everything from dim sum to French toast. I smirked at S as he examined my ridiculously full plates, and we sat down at the table. I pulled out my phone and opened Instagram, holding up the screen as I crammed a piece of toast into a tiny jar of jam.

"Five hundred thousand in an hour. Not bad."

"Damn, that's a lot," S said, chewing on a piece of dim sum.

I nodded and ate my toast, watching the sales of the bikini rise. We'd made a decent amount of cash and added three thousand new followers to the brand's account, and the US wasn't even awake yet. I didn't bother to check the count of my own followers. I didn't need to; I knew that whenever I posted something sexy, I'd lose some of them. The next day, however, without fail, a wave of new followers would arrive.

I'm still addicted to the sensation I get watching a post go crazy with comments and likes on Instagram. Casually snapping a picture and uploading it for 28 million people provides a pretty serious high. There's a thrill in knowing that folks all over the world might be

talking about what I posted. It's quite a rush to create
a tidal wave like that whenever I want.

For better or worse, I've always been drawn to
overexposure. Making myself big gives me a sense of
security. Be the loudest in the room, the most opin-
ionated, the one in the most revealing dress. *Do the
most*. Being big also means becoming a target. But by
inviting people's gaze and attention and therefore their
attacks, I have a sense of more power, less vulnerabil-
ity, since I'm the one putting myself out there. Or at
least that's how it feels, some of the time.

I was getting paid to take this vacation with S. A
large hotel conglomerate had just opened a new luxury
resort in the Maldives. The hotel cost $400 million to
build. The island was owned by some super-rich guy
from Qatar, we learned from the general manager, a
French man wearing all white who came and found
us at breakfast. The hotel group needed to generate
awareness, and having me visit and tag their account
and the location was valuable to them. For this kind of
advertisement, I was able to make a shit ton of money
just by vacationing here for five days and posting the
occasional picture.

The rain stopped just long enough for the ten-
minute ride back to our room. As we cycled slowly
over the wet white sand, employees in starched uni-
forms paused their raking to hold their hands together
up to their chests and bow their heads slightly. I nodded and smiled in return.

The fuzziness I'd felt earlier while watching the storm from our bed was developing into a full-on headache. I lay down and poured myself a big glass of water, unlocking my phone to check my post again: 789,357 likes. I moved my thumb down the screen and saw the number refresh. 791,476. I looked over at S, who was scrolling through Twitter. Even in this exotic setting, we could not stay away from our screens. The backs of my eye sockets throbbed. I felt a distinct impulse to throw my phone into the turquoise ocean in front of us. Instead, I buried myself in the poofy white pillows.

Next to the bed was Demi Moore's memoir, *Inside Out*. I'd finished it the night before, S sleeping beside me as I read. Demi's final message to the reader stuck with me: "Maybe some part of this story is yours, too." *I sure as hell hope not*, I thought. But she was right, even if she couldn't have known how directly some aspects of her life resembled mine—for instance, the way she used her body to succeed.

Now, I studied her black-and-white portrait on the cover, feeling annoyed with myself. I'd judged Demi before reading her book. I thought of her as sexy and not much else. *You of all people. You who just posted your ass on Instagram and have the audacity to bitch about the world not taking you seriously? What a fucking hypocrite*. I wanted to be able to have my Instagram hustle, selling bikinis and whatever else, while also being respected for my ideas and politics and well, everything besides my body. I pressed my fingers into my forehead and shut my eyes tightly. Everything felt like a mistake: my stay in this bizarrely perfect environment, the followers seeing my image and judging it. *At what cost did this vacation come?* I was getting paid by a corporation owned by some billionaire (*who made his fortune how, exactly?*) and posting images that encouraged the world to see my body as my primary value. *It's my fault.* My stomach tightened. *Maybe I should jump in the ocean,* I thought. *Purify myself in the rain and salt water.*

I was born a year after Demi starred in *Ghost,* the film that propelled her to fame. By the time I could read tabloid covers in the checkout line, her time as a respected actress had morphed into something else, and I absorbed the idea that she was more interesting for her love life than her acting. I remembered her in *Charlie's Angels,* climbing out of the water in a black bikini. I'd always thought of her as beautiful, sure, but certainly not as serious. I'd only picked up Demi's book because I'd read her co-writer's memoir and liked it.

I texted my friend Jessica. "Fuck, even I have internalized misogyny." Jessica and I exchanged texts like this regularly. She'd get it. Or maybe not? Jessica came from money, and I wasn't sure if she'd ever even considered capitalizing on her body in the way that I've done. Then again, she'd married a much older and financially successful man when she was very young. *Model or influencer or actor or not, all women know what it's like to use their sexuality for security in some capacity*, I thought. Anyway, it was the middle of the night where she was. I fought the urge to go back to Instagram to check my likes and comments. I dropped the phone on the ground next to the bed and turned to S, my headache pounding.

Later, the sun broke through the clouds and we headed down to the beach, bringing a bag full of books and our iPhones. We dipped in the warm ocean and floated in the salty water, far from everything and everyone back home. I brought my legs around S's torso, feeling the weightlessness of my body in the water. We kissed and marveled at our surroundings. The big sky wrapped around us.

"Being here makes me think a lot about money," S said once we'd returned to our beach chairs and as he sprayed white sunscreen onto his face. I inspected the other guests from behind my sunglasses.

"Rich people," I muttered as we began to speculate. How did they even decide where they were going on vacation? Did they go to the same places again and again? Did their kids fly first-class, too? How much would this vacation of ours cost, anyway? We tallied the prices of the flights, the drinks, the meals.

"Damn," I said. "This shit is rich as fuck."

"Yeah, but we're living it, baby. We're living like really rich people."

I tugged my hat brim down to shade the tip of my nose as I reached for my piña colada.

"But I played the system," I said, taking a big sip of alcohol. I felt the sweetness rush between my teeth. S made a face.

"What do you mean?" he asked.

I pointed out that we weren't like the other guests at this resort. "We wouldn't spend our own money to come here. It's too expensive. These people, they could shut off their phones if they wanted to," I said. "And what about the owner of the island? Or the hotel conglomerate? The money I'm making here is a drop in the bucket of their four hundred million. It's insignificant, even laughable, next to the net worth of the guy who owns the property! I'm here as a pawn, here to help *their* business. I'm an advertisement, not a vacationing guest."

S slowly cracked a smile, the lines around his eyes showing. "C'mon, baby," he said, reaching out a finger to tickle my armpit. "You're a capitalist, too, admit it."

I wriggled away, slightly annoyed. I took a gulp of piña colada too quickly and felt my sinuses burn from the sudden chill.

"I'm trying to succeed in a capitalist system." I pinched the bridge of my nose. "But that doesn't mean I *like* the game. Like I said, I worked the system." S shook his head and let out a chuckle, rubbing more sunscreen onto his arm.

I searched through the screenshots saved on my phone and held it up to him. He squinted to read out loud: "'Fuck capitalism, but until it's fucked, keep getting that bag.'"

"Whatever you say." He laughed.

I looked down at my stomach, adjusting the top of my bikini. At least this paid vacation (or job, or whatever one wanted to call it) gave me the chance to push my own brand, which I'd started, financed, and now operated with only the help of Kat, who owned a percentage of the company. Kat was a senior at my high school when I was a freshman, and when I moved to New York, we'd reconnected and become close friends. She'd worked in fashion for years before she joined me. Kat's boyfriend was almost ten years older than she, divorced with two kids. He managed a real estate investment trust and owned several homes. When he'd ask Kat about business, she didn't like to answer or give specific numbers. "It's just weird," she whispered to me, even though no one else was around. "It's like, I don't want to tell him anything until, like, we can really blow his mind. You know? He's *in* it. One of the boys. I don't want to be the girls running a *cute* business. I want to fuck them all up."

I knew what she meant. I also wanted to be someone men like that couldn't dismiss. While I wasn't at all interested in becoming a girlboss type, I figured it would be stupid to use my body to promote some rich guy's bikini line instead of my own.

One of my favorite pieces of art is by a woman named Hannah Black. She's mostly a writer, but she occasionally creates work that is political, and the one that I love is an audio recording. You can hear it online—it's accessible to everyone. The whole piece is comprised of famous women singers, mainly black, singing the words "my body" over and over. Rihanna, Beyoncé, Whitney. The two-second clips play on a loop: "My body. My body! My bow-day!"

"My body!" I sang out loud in my best Rihanna voice, thinking of Hannah Black's piece as I stepped into the water, adjusting my wet bikini bottom to wedge it farther up my ass. The image of Halle Berry emerging from the surf in *Die Another Day* came to mind. *Halle Berry was hot*, I thought, yet she only managed to win an Oscar by making herself look ugly, in *Monster's Ball*. I remembered what my agent had told me. "If you want people to think of you as a good actress, you're going to need to get ugly." She'd said it as if it were obvious. I felt a sudden urge to cover myself up.

Just a month earlier, Jessica had sent me a quote of Halle's via DM. "My looks haven't spared me one hardship," it read.

"The funny thing abt this is at first it really pissed me off bc he-llo HALLE BERRY!?" Jessica had written. "But then I started thinking about your life and how I'd assumed you had everything I could ever want bc of the way you look. But obviously I now know that's not true. It's not true for any woman! Even if you're Halle fucking Berry. As a woman I'm always thinking if only my ass was a little tighter or my nose was a little smaller my whole life would be different if only I made myself more appealing to men."

*Bc he-llo HALLE BERRY,* I repeated in my head. Did this vacation perfectly disprove Halle's point? But then why did I feel so uneasy? The contract I'd signed with the hotel lurked in the back of my mind. I was dizzy—from the alcohol or the sun, I wasn't sure.

Back in my chair, I opened Instagram to a new post from a young actor. She was wearing a turtleneck dress, with her brown hair parted neatly to the side like a 1940s movie star, a diamond stud in her ear. She was beautiful, this girl, Rachel. I'd known her for several years, from way back when she was blond. We'd met on the set of a catalog job for a big clothing company.

I liked her right away, even though I found her attitude a bit too chirpy. Work was work to me, not fun, even if the shoot was glamorous, but she was energetic and chatty, trying hard to charm the client and the other models. She sipped Evian through a straw as she told me all about her stepfather, a man thirty years her mother's senior and one of the biggest actors of my parents' generation. When she went to the bathroom, the hairdresser tsk-tsked, curling my hair around a hot iron and muttering acidly, to me or maybe to himself, "Of *course* Daddy is famous." I watched Rachel in the reflection of the mirror as she returned, meeting my eyes, her full lips parted in a smile.

I next saw her at a fancy Hollywood party. We sat

together for a moment at the edge of the dance floor, as she talked about her burgeoning acting career. "I mean, it sucks, anyone who googles me, the first thing they see are my tits in a bikini photoshoot from, like, four years ago." Rachel seemed shockingly childlike at times, prone to spurts of animated excitement—the way she bounced around the party asking anyone and everyone how her hair looked. At other moments, she seemed older and more composed, never missing a beat with social cues, her smile and cadence perfectly timed and delivered.

Her eyes scanned the party as she continued, "I mean you're lucky, with your whole political thing, being outspoken and supporting Bernie, all that stuff, I think people take you more seriously," she went on, generously.

*No one takes me seriously*, I wanted to whisper, but she was up and off again, screaming and sprinting toward an arriving guest.

I watched Rachel's transformation over the years via Instagram. The turtleneck dress seemed like a culmination: no more sexy stuff for her. *Is that the way to be taken seriously?* I wondered. *Covering up your body and dressing like you're going to see the Queen of England?* Would this ensure a career with longevity? Maybe, but it didn't seem fair that she should have to start wearing sweaters and dyeing her hair brown to be considered serious.

A large group approached from the left side of the long white beach. Four women, all dressed in long-sleeved black tops and pants and skirts and head-scarves, talked among themselves, gazing down at their feet in the sand. They walked behind a group of men who were smoking and drinking out of big glasses like mine; they were shirtless and in short swimming trunks. The women stopped at the water's edge and sat in a row in the surf, their clothing instantly heavy with the weight of the water. The black fabric pooled around them. I watched their silhouettes against the bright sand and the big blue sky. They had their backs to me, gesturing to one another and only occasionally glancing toward the men, who were now at the bar. I wondered what they were talking about, there at the place where the land meets the sea.

I refreshed my post. "One million likes and count-ing." I turned to S, smiling a goofy grin.

He laughed and shook his head, then returned to his science fiction book.

Back on my phone, I focused on the image of my body, the four women blurry in my peripheral vision. I scrolled down to read the most recent comment: "Men like mystery, stop showing your body and maybe someone will start listening to you."

I quickly swiped out of Instagram and thought about reading the book I'd brought with me, but opened the news app instead. A headline about Kim Kardashian caught my attention: "Why Kim Is Dressing Less Sexy."

I peered over the edge of my iPhone to check on the four Muslim ladies. *Still there*, I thought. I took another sip of piña colada and sprayed a splotch of sunscreen onto my legs, feeling my pulse in my temples. That damn headache wouldn't go away.

On my screen, Kim was saying, "I also did think, like, okay, I'm here in the White House and then the next day I was posting, like, a crazy bikini selfie. And I was thinking, I hope they don't see this, I have to go back there next week." Kim talked about her work on justice reform, how she'd realized that being sexualized wasn't helping her cause. "My husband has voiced that sometimes too sexy is just overkill." Now my sinuses were starting to ache. I once heard that headaches come from the brain swelling and pressing against your skull. This one felt exactly like that.

I spread my arms and legs out wide and closed my eyes and told myself to relax. *Money means power*, I thought. *And by capitalizing on my sexuality I have money. The whole damn system is corrupt and anyone who participates is just as guilty as I am. What am I going to do? Go live off the grid? I have to make a living somehow. Besides, I have this damn vacation that most people couldn't afford even if they saved for years. It's ridiculously expensive and I'm not even paying for it. So be grateful.*

But did I have power? Did the women on the beach in their headscarves? Did Halle Berry have more power coming out of the water as the James Bond girl or when she took off her makeup and got ugly in the film that earned her an Oscar? And did my young actor friend have more power now that she was wearing turtlenecks and tasteful diamond studs? Did Kim have more power going to the White House in her suit or when she capitalized on the release of her infamous sex tape, the one that made her the most googled woman on earth? Would anyone have cared about Kim's fight for justice reform if she hadn't had a sex tape? And why did everything these women did, what they wore and what they posted, all seem so reactive? As if they were adapting to and playing in someone else's game, with someone else's rules?

"My bow-day," I said out loud, studying the glistening skin of my hips. The whole of the ocean stretched out before me, and yet I felt trapped. My body.

# K-Spa

KOREATOWN IS SQUISHED right in the middle of a bunch of other neighborhoods: West Hollywood, Silver Lake, Mid-Wilshire, and Downtown. The clientele of the K-Town spas reflects the mixing pot that is LA. Spanish, Korean, English, Russian—the women speak their languages in hushed tones, mindful of the levels of their voices. No one wears jewelry inside the spas, and, at just $30 admission, it's difficult to tell who is rich and who isn't.

There are women with large breast implants that sit unnaturally beneath their skin; there are women with no breasts at all. There are women with scars from cosmetic surgeries, women who look like burn victims, women with faded purple lines from C-sections above their pubic hair, women stripped bare from menopause.

Some women attend in pairs, but most come alone and keep to themselves. They let their faces droop, the corners of their mouths turn down, and their eyebrows sink. What on the subway would be called resting bitch face here is just looking relaxed without pretense or performance.

Understanding and agreeing to the rules of the spa is crucial to the experience. It can take a moment to absorb those rules: Shower before you use any of the pools, keep your hair up, no bathing suits. No phones. These guidelines are posted on the wall in clear view of the entrance, laminated to guard against the steam. But the implicit rules are far more important, and come only with experience: Do not make eye contact or look directly at anyone's body. This is a place where no one is scrutinized or evaluated.

Of course, the Korean clientele are the experts; the rest of us are just students. Novices watch them out of the corners of our eyes, imitating their rituals. They are the least self-conscious and the most focused. They sit on plastic buckets turned upside down on the slippery tile floors and gaze with indifference into the small, clouded mirrors that are secured to the walls. They rub their naked bodies down with hard-textured cloths that grind and grind and grind against their skin. They wash their hair with an impressive squirt of shampoo and brush it aggressively. Sometimes they are silent; other times they speak quietly but assertively to each other in Korean. Whether they're young or old, I feel shy and juvenile in their presence. They seem to possess an inherent understanding of how to take care of themselves. There is no fussiness involved. It is what it is: they clean their bodies with matter-of-factness and purpose.

I've never been good about taking care of myself. Cleaning my body is not a habit I take pleasure in but a concession to social expectations; I know that being dirty is embarrassing and not feminine. I'm always distracted and annoyed in the shower, forgetting to shave the backs of my calves or to rinse my hair for an adequate amount of time. For me, the ritual of cleansing has always been an inconvenient necessity, something I have to do for other people.

My lack of care extends beyond hygiene. I dread doctors' appointments so much that I'm often more perturbed by having to schedule one than I am by whatever ails me. I've managed to avoid seeing a dentist for most of my twenties, a whole seven-year streak without a cleaning that I finally broke at the age of twenty-seven. I don't like the way they make me feel guilty for not flossing. When I'd tell friends about avoiding the dentist, they'd screw up their faces: "The health of your teeth is crucial, Emily!" I'd shrug, feeling a little embarrassed, a little alone, a little strange.

Yet I also frequently wake in the middle of the night worried about the condition of my teeth. I want to be healthy and alive, but I hate the inevitable question, "How long has it been since your last cleaning?"

usually asked by a stranger, likely a man. I don't want to hear him say, *You really should take better care of yourself.* I want to be the one in control of my body, even if that means denying it.

For a long time, I didn't think my body was worthy of the attention required to take care of it. I expected my body to function, but I tended to ignore it, even when it called out to me. When my right hip ached after hours of airplane travel, I wouldn't stretch my muscles. "Pain is information," my friend Sara, the kind of person who attends six a.m. yoga classes, would say to me. "Your body is trying to tell you what it needs."

But I wasn't interested in listening. If I woke up with an empty stomach, hollow and gasping for fuel, I threw bitter coffee into it instead, urging my body to function faster, move faster. I'd wait to eat until my eyesight became blurry and my hands shook and I couldn't function at all. I wasn't avoiding food; I just didn't want my physical needs to take precedence. I had no patience or time for nourishment.

I'm one with my body only during sex. When my husband and I fuck, I like to look in the mirror so I can see that I'm real. It helps me to return to myself, instead of floating above us, which happens from time to time. When I come, I finally allow myself to exist inside my body, even if only for a few seconds.

My body has been crucial to my survival; it's the tool I use to make a living as a model. But it isn't a part of my job in the way a body is for an athlete or a construction worker or the women who work at the spa. Those women are strong. They climb up on platforms and push their whole weight into the backs of other women. My body—or rather, my appearance—is an ornament used for decorating.

At the spa, we all understand that we can see each other, but we don't *look*. We're comforted by our collective nakedness. We're not here to perform. We don't have to be self-aware. Our bodies are simply undergoing maintenance. When I'm here, I'm anonymous, just another body.

I'm never self-conscious about being naked, always ready to strip. "But of course *you* are! If I had your body, I'd never have clothes on," people often say to me.

"It's just not that simple," I want to respond, but I know that then I'd have to tell them about how I dissociate when my body is being observed, how I don't even really recognize my body as *me*. "Does that make any sense?" I'd ask, and I can see them shaking their heads: *Not really.* Dissociating makes everything easier. In a way, overexposing myself has always felt like the safest option. Strip yourself naked so it seems like no one else can strip you down; hide nothing, so that no one can use your secrets to hurt you.

As IN THE spa, there are unspoken rules to being a model. On set, you learn quickly to change clothes wherever you're told to change; finding a private place wastes time, and time is money. But the expectation that models should change in front of people is also a way for the client to exert power. It's both a test and a reminder of your position: everyone else is doing their job, and now it's time for you to do yours. The stylist, their assistant, the client or editor, the other models, and sometimes the photographer will stand right in front of you and wait as you strip. You understand that your body is a means for them to accomplish what they're here to accomplish: to make an image to sell whatever it is they're selling. They're in charge of it now, not you.

*Now hand it over,* they seem to say. *Your body is why you're here and we need it. Now.* You know that *they'd* never strip down in front of ten strangers, but that's not part of their role, is it? You're the model. No one has time for your hesitation. You drop your clothes, and usually, they do not look away. In these moments, I don't hesitate. I rise to the challenge; I want to pass the test. I want to make it seem like there is no power dynamic at all, like I'm simply doing my job, like I *want* to get naked on command. I will reveal my body as naturally and uneventfully as I might do anything else. *See, nothing to hide here,* I want to say as I pull off my dress and stand naked in front of them. "I'm not afraid of your eyes." I look down at my body and it doesn't feel like my own. It feels like *something,* but not *me.* They can look at me all they want, because they're right; my body *is* just a tool.

ON MY FIRST big fashion shoot, photographed by
Bruce Weber, I changed next to Karlie Kloss in an ice-
cold trailer. A female stylist and her assistant watched
over us both. As I began to undress, I remembered my
agent's enthusiasm as she'd told me about the booking
on the phone the week before the shoot.

"This is huge!" I could feel her beaming. "Bruce
Weber! Karlie Kloss!"

"But I'll look ridiculous next to her," I said, staring
into my bathroom sink, which was no bigger than an
airplane's. I turned on the faucet and examined myself
in the mirror. "She's so much taller than me." I felt I had
to remind my agent of our seven-inch height difference.
Maybe it was something she hadn't considered? Some
part of me hoped she'd pause and say, *Oh, you're right.
I'll cancel.*

When I arrived in heels at Bruce's farm in Mon-
tauk, the sun hadn't yet fully risen. Mist surrounded
the trailer and the catering tables. I felt silly as I
poured black coffee into a paper cup, trying to balance as my heels sank into the moist grass, but I
didn't care. I was committed. I'd already decided that
I'd rather look like a fool than leave anyone with the
impression that I wasn't the right body for the job.
I wanted to prove that I belonged, that I could hold
my own.

While changing inside the trailer, I reached for my
coffee, now cold. Goosebumps covered my skin as I
stood there naked. I glanced down at my hips and legs

and handed my clothes to the stylist. She looked my body up and down. I sucked in my stomach.

"I get it now," she said. "You're *so* tiny. Like Kate Moss but with boobs." I smiled. The tool I'd brought with me was the right one.

* * *

I went to the spas in K-Town at the recommendation of my then agent, Natalie, the same year as that shoot. Natalie was blond, with short hair and smooth, nearly reflective porcelain skin. Her expression was always blank. Her no-nonsense approach to work made her a powerful agent, even militant at times. She was an authoritative figure to the "girls" she represented.

Natalie's philosophy around talking to the girls about their bodies was that it was best to be direct. She believed that a model's body is a crucial part of the job, and there was no use in being overly sensitive around the reality of the work.

When I started to make serious money as a model, the agency and Natalie paid me more attention. The first time she invited me out for dinner, I was convinced that I was in trouble. Why else would my agent take me out to dinner? I thought she wanted to discuss my weight or some other unforeseen issue with my body.

I wore a long sheer light-brown dress to meet Natalie and one of the other agents from Ford Models. I fastened a thin belt as tightly as I could around my midsection—punching new holes in the belt's fake leather with a pen and cinching it so that it dug into my flesh when I exhaled. I wanted Natalie to be able to see, right away, how small my waist was.

I pulled up to the restaurant in West Hollywood in my dirt-covered Nissan, complete with a missing hubcap and piles of clothes in the backseat from changing into appropriate outfits for castings, and tried to look adult and graceful. Natalie and her colleague were seated outside, both on the same side of a table covered in a pristine white tablecloth. They waved as I steadied myself on my heels and approached them. Everything at the restaurant felt lovely—in the way I imagined a fancy older woman might use the word—and expensive. I thought about my messy car filled with dirty coffee cups and wondered if I looked put together. As I greeted them, Natalie brought the corners of her mouth up into a smile, something I'd never seen her do before. I was surprised by how welcoming her face could be. I felt myself relax.

Over the course of our dinner, Natalie didn't bring up anything about my body and I, despite being underage and driving, drank three glasses of the driest, most delicious white wine I'd ever tasted. We talked about Los Angeles and the clients we didn't like and the clients we loved. I'd never experienced a "getting to know you" dinner with people I worked with. It was that night Natalie mentioned the Korean spa.

"You should go!" she told me, her blue eyes sparkling beneath the fringe of her blond hair. "You'll love it. It's heaven. And not at all expensive," she added, as if we were girlfriends swapping beauty tips. I smiled and nodded. Later, when I got home and undressed, I noticed red welts decorating my waist from where the belt had cut into my flesh.

* * *

I open my eyes in the Jacuzzi and step out, feeling the wrinkled soles of my wet feet against the concrete floor. My skin is moist and steaming. I'm wearing nothing but a stretchy plastic band on my wrist with a plastic tag attached to it, "23," typed in block text. This is the key to my locker and also the number the women call when they're ready for me. Then, after they're done with the scrub and massage, they'll use the stretchy band to hold my freshly washed hair away from my face.

"Twenty-three," a petite, middle-aged Korean woman calls out. Her eyes hover over the various pools until she spots me. I obediently stand up and wrap a damp towel around my body. She waits for me to come to her side and nods without really looking at me. "Hello," she says, then turns to walk through a steamy glass door. I follow behind her.

The body-scrub and massage area is lined with rows of rectangular metal platforms. They are as high as my hips and about six feet in length. Two Black women lie on adjacent platforms, washcloths placed over their eyes. The women scrubbing them move around their bodies busily, extending their arms, rubbing their thighs and glutes as they chat in Korean. The clients are silent and unmoving; their bodies jiggle passively against the silver platforms.

"Lie down," the attendant tells me, tapping a finger on the metal surface and holding out a hand to take my towel. I pass it to her, my skin slick from the steam rooms, and climb onto the platform.

The last time I'd lain on a that kind of surface was during my most recent visit to the gynecologist. I had been bleeding during sex, only after orgasm, always a week before my period. The last time it happened, I jumped off my husband and ran to the bathroom, panicked. "What's wrong with me?" I asked, tears streaming down my face as I inspected my blood on a piece of toilet paper.

In the gynecologist's office, I sat up as she asked me questions about my body. I answered straightforwardly, noticing a single bead of sweat sliding down my ribs under the paper gown I had tied under my neck. "How often has this happened? Have you had more than one partner in the last few months? Do you use protection?" She fired off question after question without looking up from her tablet.

"Is this, um, normal? Like, do you see it with a lot of people?" I said, trying to get her to meet my eyes.

"It's not unheard-of," she answered, finally putting her iPad down. "Let's take a look."

I laid my head back and felt my hands tremble. "Can you scooch your butt closer to the edge?" she asked. I obliged, wiggling my bare ass down to the end of the platform.

"There." She was focused, I noticed. "That's perfect. Now you're going to feel something cold. It might be uncomfortable. Please let me know if there's any pain."

I felt the speculum slide between my legs, and then inside of me, as my bare toes clenched in the metal stirrups. I tried to remember to breathe. I could feel the texture of the walls of my insides against the instrument's unnaturally smooth sides.

"Ahh," I made a sound as I exhaled, trying to instruct my body to unclench, but everything tightened instead.

"Is this painful?" the gynecologist asked, jolting up. I tilted my head forward. Her face was framed perfectly between my knees. I shook my head.

"Try to relax," she said. "It's normal for this to feel uncomfortable, but there shouldn't be any pain." I was suddenly embarrassed by my apparent lack of control. Why couldn't my body do what she was asking, what I wanted it to do? I smiled at her weakly.

"This always happens." I paused and then went to reassure her, "There is no pain, though." I could tell that she wasn't sure whether to believe me, that she doubted I was a reliable reporter on my own body. "I don't think it's pain," I offered, and she nodded, silent.

When I told Sara about this experience, she looked at me knowingly before I was even finished and interrupted me. "Victims of sexual assault seize up at the gyno. It's, like, a known thing." I raised my eyebrows.

"Interesting," I said, but the reason I can't relax at the doctor's office isn't because of sexual assault, or at least not exactly. For a second, I wished I could lie to Sara and point to one specific event in my past that would easily explain my body seizing up. I know that a speculum inside me reminds me of sexual violations I've experienced, sure, but I also hate the gyno because I'm not the one holding the instrument, opening myself up. I hate that I'm expected to trust someone other than myself. I hate that I am being looked at so intimately. I hate being assessed.

When I became pregnant and started to weigh the pros and cons of giving birth at home versus at a hospital, I made a list of what I feared most in each scenario. I wrote "pain" and "hemorrhaging" under home birth, and under hospital, I added "doctors and nurses." It was only then that I realized how much I'd come to distrust those in positions of power who, often without my best interests at heart and without my explicit consent, had made my body feel like it wasn't my own.

While the staff at the Korean spa are authoritative, they don't inspect and evaluate you. The terms of the service and their interaction with your body have been agreed upon in advance. They are all women. They wear minimal black undergarments that keep them cool and dry. There is a solidarity in their stripped-down attire that makes me feel safe, like we are all on the same side.

"FACE UP," THE tiny attendant tells me. A washcloth falls over my eyes.

"Thank you," I mutter, but she ignores me, already busy running hot water into a bucket. *Splash*. The water hits my body and rolls off as I quiver with pleasure.

Here at the spa, I'm not thinking about cleanliness or my insides or who I belong to. I'm just here, one of many women who are unwrapped and undressed. I've never known this kind of rest anyplace else in my life. I let my body unclench. I let myself relax. There are no binding belts or high heels or stirrups. There is no being looked at.

The scrub and massage always goes like this:

1. You lie on your back, then your side, then your other side, then your stomach. The attendant rubs a thick, fibrous rag against your skin. The sensation is somewhere between pain and a tickle. As you flip and adjust according to your body scrubber's instruction, you can peek out from under your washcloth and see the dead skin lying in neat gray rolls next to you on the metal platform. Some people are bothered by this, but I don't mind it. I see it as a sign of

progress. The attendant rubs your elbows, your ankles, your armpits, your breasts, in between your buttocks, and behind your ears, places you might not think about, with equal attention and disinterest. *Splash*.

2. Next, you are covered in a chemical-smelling soap. Bubbles multiply on your raw skin and you feel reborn. Or you just feel like a fish. *Splash*.

3. The attendant hits your back twice, firmly, with her fists. You sit up, and she tells you to stick out your hands. "Go wash," she says, squirting an exfoliating face wash into your hand. When you shower you make sure to wash your face well, as this is your only responsibility and you want to be helpful. You turn the faucet off and dry yourself with precision.

4. When you return from the shower, there will be towels draped over the metal platform. Now your attendant will beat oil into your skin using acupressure. She will hit the palms of your feet with her knuckles and pinch where your head meets your neck with all her strength. You will be kneaded and pulled and struck. I love that I can lie there and know that she's doing what she does with everyone, that unlike other places where you might be massaged, the masseuse doesn't ask you what hurts or where you need

attention. No one is pointing out a special knot or specific issue. There is no special treatment here; only exactly this ritual with no variations.

5. Your hair will be washed while you lie with a hot, wet towel draped over your entire body. Your attendant will scratch the shampoo into your scalp so hard you worry your skin will split open. But it won't, and soon you'll feel blood flow into your temples. Your hair will be brushed with determination and without mercy. This might be my favorite part.

I'm sorry to return to the white light of the locker room and the women dressing themselves and prepping to resume their lives. I dislike snapping my bra back together against my back and slipping a T-shirt over my head. As I dress, my body quickly forgets what it was like to be naked and unobserved. The women in the locker room know to keep their eyes down and not look at each other's bodies, not wanting to break the spell. I've never once been recognized at the spa, or at least no one has ever made it known that they recognize me. I slide my sneakers onto my bare feet, suffocating them, and I walk differently as soon as I have them on. I check my cell phone and answer emails as I head up, up, up to the ground level and the parking lot. I feed a validated parking ticket into a machine and start to drive, exiting the parking lot on Wilshire with the window rolled down but the radio turned off. A sense of loss overwhelms me as I leave. The silence feels right.

I pause before making a left to join the traffic, noticing a truck in my peripheral vision, blocking my turn. I sink in my seat and wait, but it doesn't move. I finally look at the driver and notice that his window is also down. He waves.

"Hey," he says. He has gaps in his top teeth. "Can I get your phone number?"

I shake my head, then pull out of the lot, using both hands to angle the steering wheel and swerve my car around the bed of his truck. I roll my eyes but I can't help but check the rearview mirror to study my face, polished and free of makeup. *I guess he thought I looked pretty*, I think. I smirk a little despite myself. I notice that my lips look pale. As I drive home, I reach into my bag and put on some lipstick.

# The Woozies

My father built the house I grew up in. Tucked away in the sprawling suburbs of North County, San Diego, on a street that was unpaved for most of my childhood, the house sits on top of a small hill in clear view of the road. If by chance my father is in the driveway getting the newspaper or returning from a walk, people driving past will roll down their windows and yell out, "Your house is amazing! It looks like something out of a fairytale."

The house is small, no more than eight hundred square feet, painted dark green and covered in ivy, with the windows and doors trimmed in white. It looks like it sprang naturally out of the yard where eucalyptus, pine, and our past Christmas trees grow, some to over twenty feet. Funky potted plants and cacti sit positioned like guards at the doorway. The house is a magical organism, a place both to absorb and be absorbed by.

The effort and consideration that went into each small detail are palpable: the stain of the golden wood floors, the mismatched doorknobs and lamps collected by my father over the years, the copper piping that clings to the beams, exposed along with the interior of the roof. The walls dividing the rooms are truncated, reaching just about halfway to the ceiling. When guests come over, they run the sink in the bathroom for privacy.

My father loves to talk about the house and how he built it. Growing up, I loved to listen, following him from room to room as he recited tales attached to its features: the full-length mirror in my bedroom that he installed for his girlfriend, a ballerina, before he met my mother; the tiny ceramic jar in the dining room that my grandfather found in the rubble of Hiroshima ("Careful, it's probably still radioactive"); the painting in my parents' bedroom fixed to the wall with a hinge that opened to reveal a hidden TV ("I just don't like the look of TVs"). Guests trip on the uneven steps that lead from the double doors ("They were Jimmy Cagney's") to the entrance to my father's studio. "You know," my mother says, partly embarrassed, partly proud, "it's an artist's house."

My father and the house were bound together. He was the architect, the groundskeeper, the historian, the author of the fairytale. Though my mother and I lived there, too, it was unmistakably his.

On many days while I was growing up, the house felt glorious; it would fill with my father's excitement over a new painting he was working on, or with my mother's joyous preparation for a visit from friends. They both enjoyed tending to the house, and at times like these, it thrived, sparkled. Sunlight appeared in places usually cast in shadow. My parents would flirt, referencing scenes from Woody Allen films they both loved and recounting stories of living in communist Poland when my mother was teaching there on a Fulbright. In the early evenings, they'd drink wine while my father blasted the Band and Van Morrison. Those nights I often woke up to the rhythmic sound of my parents having sex.

More frequently, I woke to the sound of their arguments. My father would slam the front door so forcefully the whole house shook. The rooms (if you could call them that) couldn't contain my parents' energy, much less their fighting. I was sucked into their screaming matches, positioned between them, at times literally, as they hurled cutting insults and accusations I could only partly comprehend. In an attempt at privacy, I'd close the door to my room and get down on the floor to play with imaginary friends and stuffed animals. But I could still feel the waves of tension wash over me. I'd sink like a rock dropping to the bottom of an aquarium, perfectly still. I could hear my parents' thoughts even when the house was silent. When the house was silent, it felt the loudest.

I knew that my parents had been on again, off again for years before my mother became pregnant with me and they decided to get married. I understood that even before I was born my existence was the essential glue of their relationship. After every such explosion, which usually ended with one of them leaving, the other would turn to me to plead their case or to air their grievances. I'd listen, performing my role dutifully, feeling a queasiness that would stay with me for days.

I remember sitting at the kitchen table, a glass of juice in front of me, as my mother organized printouts of exchanges between my father and various women (ex-students, former lovers, some random woman he met on a plane) that she'd found by breaking into his email.

"Is he crossing a line?" she asked.

Lines were never clear between us. The house didn't help: it was a place with no boundaries. Children who grow up in homes like mine, just them and their parents with no separation, physically or emotionally, become experts in a very particular type of seeing. We learn to see things that are hidden, and things that aren't there at all. We become particularly sensitive to the moods and emotions of others. We are nimble and excellent at shape-shifting. We oscillate between feeling special and feeling alone. We feel simultaneously capable of both saving and destroying those we love.

On some nights, I'd stare up at the underbelly of the roof and be unable to soothe my uneasy mind to sleep. I'd lie in bed, restless and sweaty, my thoughts racing. Eventually I'd call over the stunted wall between my room and my parents', at first quietly and then louder and louder, hearing the sound of my voice travel along the underbelly of the roof.

"Mom . . . Mom? Mommy!"

I'd wait, fretful and curled up until she'd come into my bed. "Do you have the woozies?" she'd ask, as hot tears streamed down my face. I'd nod and clutch at her.

*The woozies* was what I called the anxiety in my belly, because the feeling reminded me of being carsick "and a little sad," as I'd explain. We used the term regularly.

My mother had her own struggles with the woozies, something I knew from a young age. It had been so bad that she had once stayed at a hospital. She told and retold the story like a bedtime tale. "I checked myself in," she'd begin, and I'd picture her head against a stiff white pillow, her tanned arm circled by a patient wristband. I imagined my father entering hesitantly, with gift-shop flowers she wouldn't like, wrapped neatly in newspaper.

"I graded all my papers from my hospital bed and got them back to my students in time." I envisioned the thick stack of papers next to her legs, on top of the white blanket.

"We were worried you'd inherit all that, and I'm so relieved that you didn't! My depression went away when you were born. It just went away because of you."

I became used to the idea of being an antidote for both my parents. One evening, I must've been about fifteen, my mother and I were chatting in the living room. She sat curled up in her chair, which was always next to my father's. Her eyes shone as she cradled a glass of wine in her hand. Golden light fell across her nose and forehead. She was relaxed, I could tell.

"Your father and I have said if anything ever happened to you, we'd kill ourselves." She spoke matter-of-factly. "That would be it for us, there would be no reason to live." She lifted her glass and took a sip.

"I don't want to be your only reason to live," I said, haltingly, stumbling over my words. I tried again; "I don't want to hear that."

"Oh, Emily, I wasn't saying it like *that*." She clicked her tongue against the roof of her mouth. Still, I got the sense that, striking out on my own, leaving them—leaving the house—would kill them.

After I moved out, my father told me: "First it was just me in the house, then your mother, then you. Then our first dog, then a cat. Now you're gone, and the animals are dead and buried in the backyard. One day soon, we'll be dead, too, and then it'll just be the house."

* * *

My father always joked about dying early. "I won't be at your wedding," he'd say. "Big guys are like big dogs! We don't live that long." But over time, as I became twentysomething and my parents hit their sixties, it became apparent that his health was actually stellar. My mother, on the other hand, was beginning to have more and more complicated health problems with each passing year. Her father ("a small dog," my dad would have said) had lived to 103 and had not had so much as a single cavity over the course of his life. We'd always assumed that my mother's later years would be much the same as his had been. She was wiry and driven, and her hair was still thick and grew lusciously on her head. At first, her sixties seemed to suit her, as if she'd reached the age she was always meant to be. She looked like a poster child for the Golden Years: she was going to finish the book she'd been trying to write since the Berlin Wall fell in 1991 (my birth year); she was going to start working out and making new (women!) friends.

But instead of long lunches with these friends or afternoons spent writing at her desk, she became increasingly preoccupied with arranging medical tests and meetings with specialists, trying to find ways to manage the pain she had begun to feel in her back and hips. Doctors were quick to diagnose and cut open my mother's body: she had three hip replacements and neck and back surgery in five years. It seemed every ailment led only to more complications. As her energy faded and her pace slowed, she became steadily more infirm, depressed, and confused.

The first sign of a grave illness appeared in my mother's hands, which began to go numb in her sleep. I'd always admired her hands; they were the same as her mother's hands: elegantly shaped and feminine without being dainty. I have a version of them, too. She'd wake up to find them curled into each other and close to her face, arms braided together on her chest. She was folding into herself like a flower in a time-lapse video, collapsing in an unnatural rhythm.

Next came the blisters, bold and dark and hard. They appeared when she used her hands: she'd open a jar and an angry-looking blister would show up on the inside of her thumb. Press a button too hard and a blister would emerge at the tip of her finger, purple and flat.

I'd wake often in the middle of the night, worrying, and turn to the task of attempting to diagnose my mother's illness. I'd search "blisters on hands" and find myself looking at dire WebMD descriptions and frightening images of old men with deep purple circles around their eyes.

After years of my mother accumulating bizarre symptoms, for which her doctors in San Diego offered contradictory diagnoses, my parents and I resolved to go to the Mayo Clinic in Rochester, Minnesota, to see if someone could make sense of her condition. My parents flew in from California and I from New York, where I was living at the time. My mother had booked one room with two full-sized beds, in hopes I would share with them, but I insisted on my own room the day before I arrived. We met at dawn in the hotel lobby, where we picked at dry banana bread wrapped in cellophane.

That first day, my parents walked around the facility in a haze, bewildered by the scale of the operation. My mother carried binders filled with test results and Wikipedia printouts and lists of questions stuffed into a big canvas tote that dwarfed her small frame. I stayed a few paces ahead, holding our schedule and guiding my parents to the right elevator, to take us to the right floor, to get us to the right wing, and so on. I welcomed the distraction provided by the role of manager.

As we trailed through the hospital, my mother called out, "Ems! Remember the fairground?" I looked back and nodded.

It was June and I was six when my parents brought me to the massive annual San Diego fair. As night descended after an afternoon spent petting farm animals and riding the Ferris wheel, they decided it was time to go, but were unable to find the exit. I remembered the panic I'd felt watching my father's silhouette in the dark as he began to climb a wire fence into a large and swampy bird sanctuary. I called out, my voice confident and sure, "No, Dad! Not that way," before leading them back toward the colorful lights, over a bridge, past the rides and food stalls, to the parking lot, where I eventually located their car. "You've always been so good at navigating your hopeless parents," my mother said, laughing appreciatively.

By our third day of appointments and several nights of restlessness, despite my best efforts to remain busy in the role of organizer, I could feel the woozies creeping over me. As we arrived at the next specialist's office, I knew we were inching closer to some revelation. I panicked, sensing that I was beginning to lose the composure I'd held on to since I'd landed. I wanted answers, so why did I feel as if I were about to melt into the beige linoleum floor?

I carefully lowered myself into a chair, trying to slow my breathing. I was relieved that no one seemed to have noticed I was cracking. My father sat next to me with his hands clasped between his knees, face forward, and my mother perched on the examination table. Waiting there, she looked like a little kid, her posture upright and her feet dangling and twisting together. I wanted to hug her.

When the young doctor tilted my mother's head back and directed a light at her closed eyelids, the room moved in on me. There they were: the yellow and purple circles I'd seen in Google images, described online as "raccoon eyes."

"You don't have any eyeshadow on, right, Kathy?" he asked.

"Not eyeshadow, just some mascara," she said purposefully, like a brave, honest child confessing to an adult. I stifled a sob, picturing my mother applying mascara in the dark of the hotel room, in an attempt to make herself presentable before a day filled with doctors' inspections.

Now my mother lay on the table, eyes closed, a queen in her tomb. Her hands clasped each other across her abdomen. *That's where I was*, I thought. Twenty-seven years ago, her body had been strong enough to hold me inside it. A white spotlight lit up her face as the doctor began slicing into her eyelid for a biopsy. I stifled a whimper in my arm, but I knew she could still hear me. My father avoided my eyes as tears ran down my cheeks. When the doctor switched off the spotlight, I slipped out into the narrow hallway ahead of my parents and sobbed, feeling particularly alone.

After we returned to my parents' hotel room, my father sank into one of the beds and concentrated on scrolling through his phone. My mother curled up in the fetal position on the other bed, her back toward him.

"Amyloidosis," I read aloud from my phone, "occurs when an abnormal protein builds up in your organs through your blood and interferes with their normal function." I continued to read silently. *Many varieties of amyloidosis lead to life-threatening organ failure. Treatment can help, but this condition can't be cured.*

I lay down next to my mother and began reading

her positive testimonials about treatment, to give her hope, and extreme cases, to show that her situation could be much worse. We were lucky that the protein had gone to her hands instead of her heart or kidneys, I noted. She placed her hand on my arm, listening intently and watching me. "Oh wow. Well, I guess I just feel grateful we know what it is now," she said. Eventually she fell asleep, her mouth open, her breathing steady. I put the phone down and studied her face, her delicate features textured with fine lines and the occasional subtle brown sunspot. Her thick gray hair, so soft, framed her face. I brushed a tuft off her forehead and thought about the way she looked when she cried, how her brow knitted together and up, and the way her chin quivered like an upset infant's. Something in her face had always kept a tender naïveté.

I turned away from her and lay on my back, listening to her breathing beside me. My father had fallen asleep, too, on the other bed. The walls of the hotel room inhaled and exhaled along with them, and I slipped into semiconsciousness. I thought of my mother's belief that spaces hold memories, that walls take on meaning, that homes become a part of us, just as people do. I imagined her, young and strong, in all the rooms she had known. I wondered whether the more I became a woman and the more space I occupied apart from her, the more she would deteriorate. We slept.

* * *

When my father first came to see the house I bought myself in Los Angeles, the one filled with light, he chuckled. "It's so similar to ours! Even some of the same trees! Look at the wood beams!" I looked around with a new awareness, shocked by the accuracy of his observation. *Still*, I thought, *my house has walls that meet the ceiling.*

S came with me to Los Angeles the week my mother began chemo. I'd purchased the house just a few months after we got married, but we hadn't spent much time there together yet, as I had been traveling for work and S had been based on the East Coast. On arrival, we found a hummingbird nest right above the front door, coiled around a delicate piece of ivy. We hugged each other and smiled: This was a sign. The birds were a blessing on our home, our union. How clever and magical that they'd chosen to shelter on top of our door frame!

S had returned to New York for work when I found one of the chicks on the front steps, fallen from the nest but alive. I could feel its fragility just by looking at it, the hollowness of its bones, the tenderness of its pinfeathers. I was sure that its fall had been a mistake, a small misunderstanding by the universe. I carefully— with a large leaf, never touching it directly—put the baby back in its nest.

The next day, I saw a dark shape on our white patio

steps. I shook off a feeling of helplessness and gracelessly placed the little body back in its place beside its squawking sibling—once, twice, three times. It became a part of my routine around the house: do the dishes, take out the trash, check the mail, save the baby hummingbird.

A few days later, I found the hummingbird's tiny carcass covered in ants. I used a piece of mail to sweep it off the stairs and into the plants in our front yard.

"I couldn't manage to rescue it," I told S on the phone. "I guess I'm no savior."

As MY MOTHER'S chemo began, I visited my parents' house a few times, returning to Los Angeles to sleep in my own bed after each trip. On days I was not there, my mother would call and, in a voice that sounded more like *her* mother's than her own, describe how she was feeling. She told me about a friend who had survived breast cancer: "Her girls moved back home to be with her," she said. I pictured her in her chair in the living room and the dappled sunlight coming through the window behind her.

I wasn't working on anything that demanded I be on the East Coast, and being in Los Angeles, two hours away from my mother by car, seemed like the best compromise between what I knew she wanted, which was for me to return to their house as her caretaker, and what I wanted but was too ashamed to admit even to myself, which was to be all the way across the country in my new life with S. Although I'd planned to visit her frequently, weeks passed, and I found myself staying away, afraid of the power my mother bestowed on me. I stayed in my new home alone, feeling stuck and unsure and heavy with guilt, constantly aware of the magnetic pull of my parents' house.

On these mornings, I'd wake up on our giant, hard mattress and stare at nothing. I could spend the whole day like that, watching the light cross the room until it faded. *The woozies,* I'd think. I had plans for this house, this room, and the well-lit lovemaking and strong bitter coffee S and I would share. But those plans seemed beyond reach now, as if they'd existed in someone else's life.

I wore S's musty, oversized T-shirts so that I could feel swallowed up by him, surrounded by him, but they only reminded me of my loneliness. S would text or call, but I didn't want to hear about his day or what was going on with his work. I'd end our calls bitterly, immediately regretting the tension I'd created between us. It didn't occur to me that what I wanted from S was the same thing that my mother craved from me: to have someone live in her pain with her.

After a few weeks, remembering the version of myself who'd expertly guided my parents through the Mayo Clinic, I decided to try to shake the woozies by retiling the upstairs shower on my own. The burgundy tile left behind by the previous owners looked drab and unfamiliar. I researched instructions, filled a shopping cart full of tools, considered tile patterns. *This is how you make a home yours*, I thought; *you build it yourself*. I argued with S when he said I'd need a tool called a diamond saw in order to do this, and then I gave up the plan completely.

*I'm no builder*. The house got messy instead. I stopped cleaning the coffee grounds off the counter, stopped removing dead flowers from their vases. If I spilled something, I left it there to stain. Ants took over various surfaces in the house. There was no care left in me.

When my oldest friend, Barbara—an actual caretaking expert, a preschool teacher—came to visit, she ran the bath in that drab bathroom and poured a bag of Epsom salts into it. She lit candles and scrubbed surfaces and kept close but not too close. *This is what S is supposed to be doing*, I thought indignantly. A moment passed. *No, this is what* I'm *supposed to be doing*.

At Barbara's urging, we went down to see my mother. "If it will bring you some kind of peace, why not?" she said. I drove fast. When we got there, my mother did not get off the white couch. The grandfather clock chimed on the wall, and the various greens from the front lawn shape-shifted outside. Her skin felt soft and delicate when I brushed my cheek against hers. I could tell she wasn't happy that I hadn't come on my own. She told us that she wanted to stay inside, out of the sun, so we kept the doors closed. I sat on my mother's chair in the living room and let my feet turn cold against the white tile.

Barbara led the conversation. She asked about my mother's treatment before talking about her own life and family. My mother wore out quickly. "The chemo," she said. "Girls, I'm just so tired." Her eyes grew heavy, her jaw slack. We left as she fell asleep. I called S on the ride home, but I had no words.

That night, Barbara announced that we would watch a show, one I would really like, she promised. She wrapped a blanket around me, made hot tea, and put my feet in her lap. My face was salty and puffy and red. Barbara picked an episode. Five men appeared on the TV screen: fixers come to repair another man's house and his life, too. My chest was hot from the tea. The man's wife had just died, he told the camera. We both felt it immediately: a heavy and determined sadness, the kind that was floating over my parents' house like a giant bubble. It was all over this man's house, too. Barbara looked at me: *Shit*.

I laughed and I couldn't stop.

\* \* \*

While in the hospital for sixteen days, my mother only craves baked potatoes with "the works," she tells me. I find myself with S at a fancy restaurant, ordering a single baked potato. He laughs at me. "Good order," he says, kissing my cheek. I'm devouring this potato when my phone lights up, a message from my father: a drawing. My mother is bald in this portrait, the top of her head drawn with a single confident mark. It is perfect, this crescent.

His sketches are brutally rendered. Without warning, they arrive on my phone at all hours of the day for over a month. In one my mother is sleeping, her head resting against a pillow, her cheeks bloated and her eyes two dark holes. She looks dead. I want to tell him to stop sending me these painful portraits, that I can't handle them, but I don't. Where will they go if I'm not there to receive them?

My father doesn't communicate much with me beyond his drawings and short staccato texts. They are cryptic, and punctuated in a way that makes them feel like knife jabs. I am his diary. He counts the days of what he calls "house arrest." "Day 17," he texts me. "Day 20."

One morning, I try to fall back to sleep after one of these texts arrives, but bright sunlight is streaming through my bedroom window. I think of the house I grew up in, the Georgian windows and the exposed golden-brown beams. The tiny treasures in every corner.

Framed pictures. Wood ceilings. White walls. Bookshelves. No space. Cool shadows. An image arises: I am in the living room, on the white couch, looking out at the neon-green lawn. A thick tube descends through a pane of the window, attaching itself to the side of my neck like an artery. This is my mother's love for me, I realize.

When my mother checks out of the hospital, I text her a link to a poem by Marge Piercy, "My Mother's Body." "Most important," I write, knowing that she might not feel able to read the whole poem, "is this."

> *I carry you in me like an embryo*
> *As once you carried me.*

I copy lines from a different stanza into the notes on my phone, though—one I cannot stop thinking about but will never share with her:

> *What is it we turn from, what is it we fear?*
> *Did I truly think you could put me back inside?*
> *Did I think I would fall into you as into a molten*
> *furnace and be recast, that I would become you?*

The day after Barbara leaves, I wake up surrounded by white light and march purposefully up the stairs to the bathroom with the inherited tile. I pull back the shower curtain. Barbara has left eucalyptus leaves hanging from the shower head. I inhale deeply and run the water.

I am determined to take care of myself. I am determined to make this new house my own.

The tub isn't deep enough for fully submerging

myself, but my body fits, cocooned in warm water, if I lie in just the right position: on my back, with knees bent to one side. My skin is slick and hot. I look up to where light creeps through a strip of window at the very top of the shower. This isn't the tile of my choosing, I think. But that's okay for now.

# Transactions

———

IN 2014 MY manager at the time, Evan, informed me that the billionaire financier behind *Wolf of Wall Street* was offering to pay me $25,000 to go to the Super Bowl with him. To be paid $25,000 to show up to an event that people saved money to afford was the most ridiculous thing I'd ever heard. I'd only just started to see numbers like that get thrown around, and only for jobs that required actual time and effort on my part: days of twelve-hour shoots with few breaks. I hadn't done more than a few paid appearances, and those all had talking points and a product to sell. This was different. He explained that this person, Jho Low, "just liked to have famous men and women around" and there would be other celebrities going, too. "Everybody who is anybody is doing these kinds of deals with him," he assured me. "He's just one of those insanely rich guys from Asia." Jho Low's fortune came from family money, Evan said. Easy money was a new concept, and it felt almost badass to be taking money from someone who had so much of it in return for so little.

When I searched online there wasn't much to find except a few pictures of him looking sweaty in nightclubs with Paris Hilton and some vague information about his production company.

"I'm sure Leo will be there, and a bunch of other people you'll know, or, er, recognize. You know their movie is up for five Academy Awards next month?" I could tell Evan was excited about the idea of going to the Super Bowl with this crew.

"I don't have to, like, do anything *specific*, right?" I asked. Was being at the Super Bowl my only task or was there some other more covert expectation? Evan told me he'd insisted to Jho Low's contact (another question: Whose job was it to call up celebrities' managers to get them to go to events with your boss for a fee?) that he accompany me, "Just to make sure you feel comfortable. You mind if I bring a date, too?" That was fine. I knew Evan was coming along as a chaperone or a buffer; but what he was protecting me from exactly, I wasn't sure. The money, which he would commission at ten percent, would be wired ahead of time. "I'll make sure it hits before Friday," Evan promised.

I couldn't remember what team the Seattle Seahawks were playing, only that my dad had said on the phone the day before that it should be a "good game." I'd never cared about football, but my father did. When I told him I was going, he yelped, "Ah, Emily! I'm so jealous!"

It was February, and as a recent transplant from the West Coast, I didn't have a proper coat to wear outside at a football game in the winter. My modeling agent managed to call in a favor and get hold of a white Moncler jacket for me. It was lent just for the weekend, to be returned early on Monday morning. "Don't get anything on it or they'll make you pay for it. They're a *fortune*," she warned.

Evan had suggested I hire a professional hair and makeup team for the game, but I decided not to spend the money. Instead, I tried to replicate what they did for red-carpet events: I put on more makeup than I usually wore and secured a janky hair extension to the back of my head. There would be no photographers, so I was grooming myself for just one person: the mysterious Jho Low.

We'd been instructed to meet at the Plaza, where we were directed immediately onto a bus. Evan had been right about the other guests: there were two famous models whom I'd never met before, one known for her recent appearance on the cover of *Sports Illustrated*'s swimsuit edition and the other for her stint as a Victoria's Secret angel. There were a few male actors, accompanied by their posses. The rest of the group was composed of people who seemed to work for Jho Low.

He boarded the bus last, wearing a hooded puffer. Although I had seen his picture online, I was surprised by how young he looked in person, younger than 31. As his short, pudgy frame moved down the aisle, Evan jumped up to introduce me. Was it part of the job to act excited? I mustered some enthusiasm.

"Thanks so much for having me," I offered, smiling up at him.

"Yeah, yeah, sure, sure." He nodded and grinned distractedly before taking a seat in the back.

Several police cars and motorcycles appeared, surrounding the bus. Over the rap music playing from a speaker, Evan explained that we were being escorted to the stadium to avoid traffic. "The city shuts down an avenue so that people who can afford it get this treatment." He chuckled, shaking his head. "Nuts, right?"

"Only way to do it," a small man cut in, introducing himself as Riza. "I produced *The Wolf of Wall Street* with Jho Low," he said. He took a seat across the aisle.

As an adolescent, wealth was an abstract concept to me. I had a rough idea of my parents' income, but I'd been clueless enough to ask my mother only a year earlier if forty thousand dollars was a reasonable amount for a person to live on for a year. "That's certainly not enough money to be *comfortable*," she'd said, without expounding further. I was not yet able to grasp the difference between rich fathers from my hometown and billionaires like Jho Low. There were no tiers when it came to rich people; to me, rich was just rich.

I started making my own money at fourteen. I thought it important to never be indebted to anyone. In high school, I once paid for a date with a boy I wasn't interested in, just to ensure that I wouldn't have to go out with him again or, my worst fear, owe him something sexually. I didn't have my driver's license yet, and I was concerned that I'd have to repay my date for picking me up; I offered to pay for his gas money. I plunked down a wad of cash at the Mexican restaurant where we ate. "Really, it's no problem. It was super nice of you to pick me up," I said. Paying made me feel that I was in control. I'd prided myself on being free of obligation.

* * *

When I moved to LA and started working full-time, there was a girl, Isabella, who had a look similar to mine: thick brown eyebrows and big features. Even though we were both nineteen, I felt older than Isabella. She was soft-spoken and timid, using her long hair to cover her body. We'd see each other frequently at castings, where we bonded over the loneliness of living in a new city. She told me she'd recently started going out to clubs with her housemate, Chloe, a blond model who was almost six feet tall. "You should come with us sometime," she offered.

I'd only spent a handful of nights in clubs, but I knew

that I didn't particularly enjoy them. I didn't like the music they played or how drinks spilled on my bare legs or someone always seemed to be groping me. Still, it seemed stupid to turn down an opportunity to meet new people. I was desperate to start an adult's life in Los Angeles. We made plans for the following week.

We met at a Japanese restaurant that felt more like it belonged in Las Vegas than in Los Angeles. I told Chloe and Isabella that I was nervous because I'd lost my fake ID. Chloe laughed and reassured me: "You don't have to worry about anything like that."

A short man in his midthirties, wearing a black button-down shirt, greeted us at the entrance to a private dining room, kissing Chloe and Isabella. I was surprised—I'd assumed we'd be going out with people closer to our age. He smiled widely and introduced himself to me as "Sacha, Chloe's friend," telling me to drink and eat whatever I wanted. Unfamiliar with extensive cocktail lists, I blanked when the waiter came for my order, and asked for a tequila sunrise, a drink I remembered my mother liking. The sweetness of the grenadine made me feel nauseous. As dish after steaming dish theatrically appeared on a long table, underage models trickled in, smiling nervously as Sacha stood up to greet them.

"What do you need, ladies?" he asked every time, signaling to a waiter. He was animated and anxious, unable to sit still.

"What up, Sach!" a woman dressed in chunky heels

and a leather jacket hollered as she strutted over to the private dining room. Sacha popped up. "Kim! Gorgeous as always."

Kim was our age, but it was clear that she was different, confident and at ease, a veteran. She wrapped her arms loosely around Sacha, placing her chin in the crook of his neck, and surveyed the table of quiet young women, assessing us, her gaze jumping from one to the next.

"The guys are almost here," she whispered, pulling away from him and taking a seat. Not long after that, Sacha announced it was time to leave. The long table was still covered with full plates of food. When I stayed seated, waiting for a check to appear, Isabella whispered to me, "No, no, no. We just go." Realizing that someone else was paying, I felt a twinge of uneasiness.

Outside, Sacha directed us to several black SUVs and told us to "hop in." As I climbed in, using one hand to hold down my short dress to keep it from riding up over my ass, I saw several men around the age of forty already in the car. "Hello," said a big, bald man who appeared too large for his seat. His massive hand sat heavily on the thigh of a petite, pale woman who seemed just a few years older than me. "This is my fiancée," he said. She waved listlessly. From the back seat, an unshaven, chubby man with a greasy nose called out, "Hi girls, let's party!"

At the club, the men kept offering us cocaine, which

they snorted with their backs to the dance floor. They ordered bottles of alcohol that arrived with sparkling flames, brought by women in black miniskirts and heavy eye makeup. The men grabbed our bodies and fed us shots and sang along to the obnoxious pop music and pumped their fists in the air. Mostly, though, Isabella and I stood around in a booth, barely swaying to the music and not speaking much. I noticed that Chloe was slouched in a corner. At some point the three of us must have managed to leave, because I woke up the next morning in Isabella's room with a pounding headache to a text: "So much fun last night! It's Sacha btw, save my number."

After that, I made a habit of ignoring Sacha's weekly texts, which were always versions of the same message: "Hiiii babe. Thursday. Big meal at Nobu tonight before we go out! Gonna be sick, roll through." When I told another model about him, she explained that Sacha was a party promoter.

"He got your number? He's never going to stop texting you, girl. The rich dudes pay him to wrangle models. They always start the nights off with a big dinner, so that girls who aren't making much cash come for a free meal."

The whole situation gave me the creeps, but when Sacha texted me along with Chloe and Isabella about a free trip to Coachella, including tickets to the festival, a place to stay, and a ride out to the desert in a limo bus, I was too excited to turn it down. The three of us pored over the lineup and circled the acts we wanted to see.

Coachella was expensive. Just the year before, I'd driven there with my best friend and spent two nights sleeping in my Nissan with the seats laid flat, parked in a hotel lot where we paid ten dollars each morning to eat cold, spongy eggs from the breakfast buffet. We'd sneaked into the festival and on our way home we found an old Starbucks gift certificate under my front seat that bought us bagels and cream cheese. It had been fun, but now I could be in the VIP section of the beer garden and the front row at the concerts. The prospect made me feel grown-up.

"I mean, if we're there together it'll be fine," Isabella texted me. We figured we could ignore the men while taking advantage of their setup.

We hit gridlock traffic leaving Los Angeles. There were about fifteen of us plus Sacha on the party bus, which was tricked out with purple neon lights and a bar filled with ice and bottles of alcohol. Sacha kept the music loud, walking the length of the aisle refilling drinks and smiling broadly. Eventually, even the most animated girls seemed to tire out. We stared at our phones. A tall model with thick black hair and a nasal voice came and sat next to me.

"So you know the big bald one is, like, a prince, right?" She melted into the seat, her long legs extending across the aisle. She was dressed straight out of the seventies: long skirt, crop top, and stacked bracelets. "His mom is super famous obviously. But yeah, I've heard him and his fiancée like to have threesomes." Grinning, she retied a colorful silk scarf around her forehead. "So they're, like, always looking for girls for those."

When we finally arrived at the massive Spanish-style house in the desert where we'd be staying, we'd been in traffic for nearly six hours and were all exhausted and ready for bed. Sacha became frantic, trying to keep us awake. "Girls! Look how dope this house is!" he squealed when we entered the foyer, grabbing at us and ordering us toward the pool in the backyard. "Go for a night swim!" Outside, we found the prince and his pale fiancée in the Jacuzzi, along with some broad-shouldered man I'd never met before. We stood uncomfortably around the edge, admiring the house. A few girls changed into their swimsuits and got in the water. When I stripped down to the bikini I'd been wearing under my denim shorts, I felt the prince's eyes land on my body.

"Okay," he said, nudging his friend. "I'm always interested in something like this." He pointed at me. "A girl like you, what do you want to change about your body? Like, what's the thing you're hung up on?" They both stared at me. I froze.

"I don't know," I responded, mentally running through the things I'd like to change about myself: a smaller nose, longer legs. He sipped his drink as his attention shifted elsewhere, bored when I didn't play along. Despite being a little scared of him, I felt a strange sense of loss. Powerful men have always had that effect on me; they make me want to be noticed but also to disappear. I watched the prince as he laughed. The lights from the Jacuzzi lit his face from below, casting grotesque shadows.

I went back inside the house. The unshaven guy with the greasy nose I'd met in LA was blasting music in the kitchen and pouring drinks, wearing sunglasses and a pink hat that had oversized bunny ears attached. I let out a small laugh at the sight of him. He looked up and shrugged. "Care to join?" He seemed goofy and self-deprecating in a way that endeared him to me, or at least made me less afraid. I threw on a hoodie and sat on a stool, bringing my knees up to my chin.

"Have some chocolate," he offered. "It's mushrooms and maybe some MDMA, mostly just a body high." He broke off a piece and popped it into his mouth. "It's mellow. Trust me, you'll feel great."

I was apprehensive, but I knew it couldn't be worse than more time with the prince. I bit off a small chunk and opened a bag of chips while he did a line of coke off the counter. He told me his wife and kids thought he was on a weekend yoga retreat in the desert.

"They have no idea. They think I'm *recharging*," he muttered, and bent over to snort another line. "Did you know I recently slept with a girl who woke up before me in the morning and *blow-dried her hair* and did her makeup and then crawled back next to me to pretend she'd been asleep?" Spit flew out of his mouth. I thought about the girl and how much she wanted to impress him, to look naturally beautiful first thing in the morning.

I could barely keep my eyes open and my jaw was tight because I'd been grinding my teeth, from either nerves or the drugs, I wasn't sure. Isabella came in from the pool and quietly said she'd found a room off the kitchen with a queen-size bed that we could share with Chloe. Hoping to leave unnoticed, we tiptoed off, found our bags piled up in the comically grand foyer, and carried them into the bedroom. The music from the pool got louder before we shut the door. Chloe face-planted onto the soft bed. Isabella brushed her teeth and I put on sweatpants, hoping we'd escaped.

But Sacha found us almost immediately. He opened our door. "What is this? Chloe!" he whined. "Chloe, wake up!"

Chloe was a party girl, but she was not one to be bossed around. "Too tired," she muttered into her pillow. He scowled at me and Isabella, knowing we were even less likely to rally.

Then Kim, the girl Sacha had greeted so warmly at the restaurant in LA, suddenly appeared behind him in nothing but a black string bikini. He turned to her, his tone shifting. "All right," he said seriously. "Remember what we talked about? I need you to go and do your thing out there." She nodded twice quickly and, without speaking a word, swiveled around and skipped out of sight.

"Jacuzzi time!" I heard her sing out. Sacha looked exhausted. He rubbed a hand against the back of his neck and head. Silently, I shut the door, wondering what I'd just witnessed. Was Sacha Kim's boss? Or were they cohorts? And what was she expected to go and do exactly?

I could not sleep that night, squished between Chloe and Isabella under a comforter that smelled stale and of someone else. I thought about the way the Jacuzzi's changing pink and green lights lit up the prince's face and how his body had appeared monstrous next to his tiny fiancée's. I realized I'd felt safer last year sleeping in my car in a crummy hotel parking lot. Isabella and I had been wrong. This was no free ride.

*　*　*

At the Super Bowl, I was surprised to find that my borrowed Moncler jacket was unnecessary. We weren't seated outside in the stands but in an indoor suite halfway up the stadium, complete with heating, a full bar, several attendants, and a lavish spread of food.

An Oscar-winning actor and his girlfriend stopped by, animating the back of the room a bit. Jho Low was quiet but beamed when the actor became loud and gregarious. The image of a king being entertained by a jester came to mind. I wondered how much Jho Low was paying him, and thought of our fees tallied in a ledger on some underling's computer. Hours passed. People looked at their phones and slouched in their seats. I hadn't realized how long the game would be, and after a glass of wine and several trips to the buffet, I was bored and exhausted. Jho Low himself seemed unenthused, staring vacantly. I wondered whether he even liked football.

Toward the end of the game, the men at the back stood up and Evan reported that we were headed to an afterparty. I was surprised and disappointed; I'd been looking forward to the end of this uncomfortable day. I asked Evan when he thought it would be okay for me to leave. He checked the time. "Probably a few more hours, let's feel it out." I'd been reminded: I was not free to come and go as I liked. I was on the clock.

The music was loud and the lights were low at the party space, a two-story lounge dripping with red velvet. Before heading upstairs to the small bar, I was careful to put the borrowed jacket behind a chair where no one could spill alcohol on it. After an hour or so, Evan finally indicated that I'd stayed long enough. I peered around. Who had released me? I placed my watered-down tequila on a table and went back downstairs to grab my coat.

As I walked toward the exit, I passed a group of people dancing. I saw that Jho Low's face had grown red and sweaty. He was drunk. A tray of shots of golden liquor appeared in front of him, and he grabbed two, handing one to the Victoria's Secret model. She had ignored me and the other guests, her attention focused on Jho Low. Now she kept her eyes locked on him as he took his shot, throwing her head back dramatically as he did, only to quickly toss the alcohol over her shoulder. When he faced her again, her eyes sparkled and the famous dimples appeared on her cheeks. *Damn*, I thought, *what a maneuver.* Laughing, she turned her back to him and bent her knees to grind her ass against his crotch. Jho Low's face lit up in delight.

When I stepped out the door into the freezing night, it dawned on me how differently she and I viewed the day. To her, it was an opportunity. As for me, I'd completely ignored the unspoken task I'd been hired to perform: to entertain the men who had paid me to be there.

I liked to think that I was different from women like her and Kim. But over time, it became harder to hold on to that distinction or even believe in its virtue. I watched models and actresses guarantee themselves financial success and careers by dating or marrying rich and famous men. The Victoria's Secret model eventually married a billionaire tech giant; other models I'd started out with saw their careers improve dramatically once they wed a pop star or became involved with a successful actor. The *Vogue* cover they thought they'd never have? After a wedding and a big diamond ring, there it was on newsstands, the model softly wrapped in her high-flying partner's arms. The world celebrates and rewards women who are chosen by powerful men.

I couldn't help but wonder whether those women were actually the smart ones, playing the game correctly. It was undeniable that there was no way to avoid the game completely: we all had to make money one way or another. So they were the hustlers, and I was—what, exactly? I posted paid Instagram ads for skincare and clothing brands owned by rich men. And I was no stranger to commodifying my physical presence, posing next to CEOs in their suits at their store openings and parties. Wasn't I hustling just like they were? Wasn't I on the same spectrum of compromise?

A few years after the Super Bowl I learned, along with the rest of the world, that Jho Low didn't come from a superrich family after all. With the help of the Malaysian prime minister (Riza's stepfather), Jho Low had stolen billions of dollars by funneling money from the Malaysian government into a fund that he managed.

He's now an international fugitive, wanted by the Malaysian, Singapore, and US authorities. Federal prosecutors seized almost a billion dollars in assets that were purchased with his stolen money: properties, yachts, artworks, and entertainment ($150 million was put into *The Wolf of Wall Street*). Leonardo DiCaprio himself had been given a Picasso and Basquiat, both of which were returned to the feds.

A week after the Super Bowl, Jho Low threw the Victoria's Secret model a lavish birthday party and gave her a heart-shaped diamond necklace engraved with her initials. It had cost \$1.3 million and, like everything else bought by Jho Low, was financed with money washed through Jho Low's fund. Eventually, she had to return an estimated \$8 million worth of jewelry. One of his gifts, a translucent baby grand piano, was not seized. It was so big that there was simply no way to take it out of her house.

# Buying Myself Back

MY MOTHER'S EX-HUSBAND, Jim (who, until I turned eight, I'd thought was my uncle), had Google alerts set for me. Every time my name appeared in the news—if you can call gossip websites "news"—he was notified immediately via email. Jim was well-meaning but an alarmist; he wished to maintain a relationship with me, and these alerts provided him with perfect opportunities to reach out.

I was walking through Tompkins Square Park with a friend and her dog and sipping a coffee when Jim's name lit up my phone. "See you're getting sued. My advice . . . ," he began. Jim was a lawyer, familiar with people calling him up to ask for legal advice and therefore used to doling out his opinion even when it wasn't solicited. "I guess this comes with the territory of being a public persona," he wrote in a follow-up text.

*I guess*, I thought.

I sat down on a bench and googled my name, discovering that I was in fact being sued, this time for posting a photo of myself on Instagram that had been taken by a paparazzo. I learned the next day from my own lawyer that despite being the unwilling subject of the photograph, I could not control what happened to it. She explained that the attorney behind the suit had been serially filing cases like this, so many that the court had labeled him a "copyright troll." "They want $150,000 in damages for your 'use' of the image," she told me, sighing heavily.

In the photo, I'm holding a gigantic vase of flowers that completely covers my face. I'd purchased the flowers for my friend Mary's birthday at a shop around the corner from my old apartment in NoHo. The arrangement was my own; I'd picked flowers from various buckets around the shop while telling the women behind the counter that a friend was turning forty. "I want this bouquet to look like her!" I'd said, grabbing a handful of lemon leaves.

I liked the shot the paparazzo got, but not because it was a good photo of me. I'm completely unrecognizable in it; only my bare legs and the big old-fashioned tweed blazer I was wearing are visible. The wild-looking flowers substitute for my head, as if the arrangement had

grown skinny legs and thrown on dirty white sneakers—a bouquet hitting the concrete streets, taking a
walk out on the town.

The next day, after I'd seen myself in the picture
online, I sent it to Mary, writing, "I wish I actually had
a flower bouquet for a head."

"*Ha!* Same," she wrote back immediately.

I posted the image to Instagram a few hours later,
placing text on top of it in bold white caps that read
"MOOD FOREVER." Since "Blurred Lines," paparazzi
have lurked outside my front door. I've become accus-
tomed to large men appearing suddenly between cars
or jumping out from around corners, with glassy black
holes where their faces should be. I posted the photograph of me using the bouquet as a shield on my Instagram because I liked what it said about my relationship
with the paparazzi, and now I was being sued for it. I've
become more familiar with seeing myself through the
paparazzi's lenses than I am with looking at myself in
the mirror.

And I have learned that my image, my reflection, is
not my own.


WHILE WE WERE together several years ago, my boyfriend befriended a guy who worked at an important
international art gallery. The gallerist said we might
want to take a look at its upcoming show of Richard

Prince's "Instagram Paintings." The "paintings" were actually just images of Instagram posts, on which the artist had commented from his account, printed on oversize canvases. There was one of me in black and white: a nude photograph of my body in profile, seated with my head in my hands, my eyes narrowed and beckoning. The photo had been taken for a magazine cover.

Everyone, especially my boyfriend, made me feel like I should be honored to have been included in the series. Richard Prince is an important artist, and the implication was that I should feel grateful to him for deeming my image worthy of a painting. *How validating.* And a part of me *was* honored. I'd studied art at UCLA and could appreciate Prince's Warholian take on Instagram. Still, I make my living off posing for photographs, and it felt strange that a big-time, fancy artist worth a lot more money than I am should be able to snatch one of my Instagram posts and sell it as his own.

The paintings were going for $80,000 apiece, and my boyfriend wanted to buy mine. At the time, I'd made just enough money to pay for half of a down payment on my first apartment with him. I was flattered by his desire to own the painting, but I didn't feel the same urge to own the piece as he did. It seemed strange to me that he or I should have to buy back a picture of myself—especially one I had posted on Instagram, which up until then had felt like the only place where I could control how I present myself to the world, a shrine to my autonomy. If I wanted to see that picture every day, I could just look at my own grid.

To my boyfriend's disappointment, his gallerist friend texted him only a few days later to say that a prominent collector wanted it.

I knew the gallerist through a bunch of different people and had met him once or twice, so it didn't take long to find out what actually happened to the piece. The giant image of me was hanging above the couch in his West Village apartment.

"It's kind of awkward," a friend of mine said, describing the painting's placement in the gallerist's home. "He, like, sits under naked you."

But it turned out Prince had made another Instagram painting of me, and this one was still available. The piece was a reproduction of a photo from my first appearance in *Sports Illustrated*. I was paid $150 for the shoot and a couple grand later, when the magazine came out, for the "usage" of my image. I hated most of the photos from that spread, because I didn't look like myself: the makeup was too heavy, there were too many extensions in my hair, and the editors had kept telling me to smile in a fake way. But I did like a few of the images of me in body paint and had posted one of those pictures, which Prince then reused for this "painting."

Prince's comment on that post, included among several others at the bottom of the painting, alludes to an imagined day he has spent with me on the beach:

"U told me the truth. U lost the [⚓]. No hurt. No upset. All energy bunny now that it's sunny," it reads. I liked the comment he left on this one far better than his comment on the black-and-white study, where he asks, "Were you built in a science lab by teenage boys?"

When I realized that my boyfriend and I had the opportunity to procure this one, it suddenly felt important to me that I own at least half of it; we decided to purchase it directly from the artist and split the cost down the middle. I liked the idea of getting into collecting art, and the Prince seemed like a smart investment. But mostly, I couldn't imagine not having a claim on something that would hang in my home. And I knew my boyfriend felt like this was some kind of conquest; he'd worked hard to get it. *I should be appreciative*, I thought. *Just split it with him.* Besides, I was twenty-three; I hadn't made enough money to comfortably spend $80,000 on art.

When the piece arrived, I was annoyed. I'd seen online that other subjects of the Instagram paintings were being given studies, the smaller drafts of the final works, as gifts. My boyfriend asked the studio, and some months later, a twenty-four-inch mounted black-and-white "study" arrived. It was a different shot than the large piece we had purchased, but I still felt victorious.

When our relationship ended, about a year and a half later, I assumed he wouldn't want the canvas—a giant picture of me, now his ex—so we began to make arrangements to divide our belongings, including the artwork we had bought together. In exchange for two other pieces of art, I received ownership of the Prince.

A few weeks later, I realized—sitting up straight, half asleep in my bed with my jaw clenched in the middle of the night—that I hadn't collected the black-and-white study the studio had given me. My ex said he "hadn't thought about that" and told me he'd moved the piece into storage. We went back and forth via email until he told me I needed to pay him $10,000 for the study, a price he'd arrived at from his "knowledge of the market."

"But it was a gift to me!" I wrote.

I reached out to Prince's studio. Could they offer some clarity or assistance? Help me get my ex to back off this ridiculous ransom? Through my contacts, I was assured that they would reach out to him to confirm that the study had been a gift from Prince to me and me alone. He didn't respond well to this assertion.

All these men, some of whom I knew intimately and others I'd never met, were debating who owned an image of me. I was considering my options when it occurred to me that my ex, whom I'd been with for three years, had countless naked pictures of me on his phone.

I thought about something that had happened a couple of years prior, when I was twenty-two. I'd been lying next to a pool under the white Los Angeles sun when a friend sent me a link to the bulletin board 4chan. Private photos of me—along with those of hundreds of other women hacked in an iCloud phishing scam—were expected to leak onto the internet. A post on 4chan listed actresses and models whose nudes would be published, and my name was on it. The pool's surface sparkled in the sunlight, nearly blinding me as I squinted to scroll through the list of ten, twenty, fifty women's names until I landed on mine. There it was, in plain text, the way I'd seen it listed before on class roll calls: so simple, like it meant nothing.

Later that week, the photos were released to the world. Pictures meant only for a person who loved me and with whom I'd felt safe—photos taken out of trust and intimacy—were now being manically shared and discussed on online forums and rated "hot" or "not." Rebecca Solnit wrote about the message that comes with revenge porn: "You thought you were a mind, but you're a body, you thought you could have a public life, but your private life is here to sabotage you, you thought you had power so let us destroy you." I'd been destroyed. I'd lost ten pounds in five days, and a chunk of hair fell out a week later, leaving a perfectly round circle of white skin on the back of my head.

The next day, I wired my ex the money. I didn't think I could survive going through what I'd been through again. I exchanged the safety of those hundreds of Emilys for one image—an image that had been taken from my platform and produced as another man's valuable and important art.

I hung the giant Instagram painting, the image from the *Sports Illustrated* shoot, on a prominent wall in my new home in Los Angeles. When people visited, they'd rush toward it and yell, "Oh, you got one of these!"

My guests would cross their arms and study the painting, read Prince's comment, and smile. The comment above his came from some unknown user; they'd often turn back to me to ask if I knew what it said. "Is it German?" they'd wonder aloud, squinting.

Eventually, after enough people asked, I decided to translate the comment myself.

"It's about how saggy my tits look," I told my husband, with whom I now share a home. He came over and put his arms around my back, whispering, "I think you're perfect." I felt myself stiffen. Even the love and appreciation of a man I trusted, I had learned, could mutate into possessiveness. I felt protective of my image. Of her. Of me.

The next time someone asked about the German comment, I lied and said I didn't know.

* * *

In 2012, my agent told me I should buy a bus ticket from Penn Station to the Catskills, where a photographer named Jonathan Leder would pick me up and reimburse me for my fare. We'd shoot in Woodstock, for some arty magazine I'd never heard of called *Darius*, and I'd spend the night at his place, she said. This was something the industry calls an unpaid editorial, meaning it would be printed in the magazine and the "exposure" would be my reward.

I had been working with my agent full-time for about two years. She had known me since I was fourteen, when I landed my first modeling and acting jobs, but she began to take my career more seriously when I turned twenty. I began to take my career more seriously, too: I dropped out of UCLA to pursue modeling and was working quite regularly. I opened an IRA and paid off my first and only year at college with the money I'd made. I wasn't doing anything fancy or important, mostly e-commerce jobs for places like Forever 21 and Nordstrom, but the money was better than what any of my friends were making as waitresses or in retail. I felt free: free of the asshole bosses my friends had to deal with, free of student-loan debt, and free to travel and eat out more and do whatever the hell I pleased. It seemed crazy to me that I had ever valued school over the financial security that modeling was beginning to provide.

When I looked up Jonathan's work online, I saw a few fashion editorials he'd shot on film. *A little boring*, I remember thinking. *Hipster-y.* His Instagram was mostly pictures of his home and a few strange, retro images of a very young-looking Russian woman with obvious breast implants. *Kind of weird*, I thought, but I had seen weirder. *Maybe this is just the stuff he puts on his Instagram?* His work on Google looked celestial and pretty. Legit. I didn't bother to investigate further. Besides, my agent was in full control of my career: I did what she told me to do, and in return, she was supposed to expand my portfolio so I could book more paid jobs and establish myself in the industry. As promised, Jonathan picked me up from the bus stop in Woodstock. He had a small frame and was plainly dressed in jeans and a T-shirt. He seemed distinctly uninterested in me and didn't meet my eyes as he drove us in a vintage car over streets lined with tall grass. He came off as a nervous, neurotic artist type. He was very different from the other "fashion" photographers I'd met up to that point, men who tended to be LA douchebags with strategically placed highlights in their hair and who smelled like sweet cologne.

I was wearing a tank top that I'd tucked into the front of high-waisted shorts, and as we drove, I watched the soft blond hairs on my thighs glisten in the sunlight. Jonathan never looked at me directly, but I remember feeling watched, aware of our proximity and my body and how I might appear from his driver's seat. The more indifferent he seemed, the more I wanted to prove myself worthy of his attention. I knew that impressing these photographers was an important part of building a good reputation. *Does he think I'm smart? Especially pretty?* I thought about all the other young models who must have come to this bus station in the Catskills and sat in this car.

When we arrived at Jonathan's home, two children

were sitting at the kitchen table. I stood awkwardly at the door in my short shorts and felt embarrassingly young—unwomanly even, like a kid myself. I noted the time from a clock on the wall: *How are we going to shoot today if it'll be dark in just an hour and a half? Maybe we'll shoot very early tomorrow*, I figured. I brought my hands up to the straps of my backpack and shifted my weight from side to side, waiting for instruction. I felt relief wash over me when a makeup artist arrived at the house and proceeded to set up on the kitchen table next to Jonathan's kids. She was older than me, and quiet. I felt more comfortable upon her arrival; the pressure was off me to know how to be and how to compensate for Jonathan's strangeness now that another adult was there, a woman.

The makeup artist finished setting up and began working on my face while Jonathan cooked dinner. He offered me a glass of red wine, which, in my nervousness and desire to seem older and wiser than I was, I accepted and drank quickly. I took deep sips as the makeup artist painted thick, black, wet liner on the tops of my eyelids. I opened my iPhone's selfie camera in my lap to check her work. She was making me look pretty, transforming me to fit Jonathan's aesthetic vision. When he laid out old-fashioned lingerie on a kitchen chair, I began to grasp what type of girl he wanted me to be. My agent hadn't mentioned that the shoot would be lingerie, but I wasn't concerned; I'd done countless lingerie shoots before. I could imagine her writing to me the next day, "Jonathan loved you. Can't wait to see pics! Xx," as she had on other occasions.

Jonathan's kids were picked up by someone who did not come inside the house, while the makeup artist finished preparing my face. When he was done cooking, Jonathan, the makeup artist, and I all sat around the kitchen table eating pasta, as if we were a small family. He talked about his "crazy" ex-wife and his affair with a "crazy" actress, now twenty-one (a year older than me, I noted). He told me about his marriage's undoing; that the actress, whom Jonathan had cast for a short film he'd been making at the time, came to live with them. He showed me naked pictures, Polaroids, he'd taken during their affair. She seemed so vulnerable in Jonathan's photos, even though I could tell she was trying to look strong and grown-up from the way she held her face square to the camera, chin up, her hair falling perfectly over one eye.

"No one has shot her better," he said over his shoulder, as I continued to riffle through the Polaroids.

Something switched inside me then. As I looked at the images, I grew competitive. *This guy shoots all these women, but I'm going to show him that I'm the sexiest and smartest of them all. That I am special.* I chewed on my lower lip as I handed the neat stack of Polaroids back to Jonathan.

I wondered where he normally kept these Polaroids. Were they all meticulously labeled in a giant filing cabinet somewhere in his attic, the names of young women written in ink on their assigned drawers? The image of a morgue came to mind.

It was dark, and my hair was still in rollers as I finished my third glass of wine, my mouth stained purple. I was used to unusual setups on shoots, but I'd never been in a situation like this before. I made sure not to eat too much, while Jonathan silently refilled my glass and I kept drinking. In the industry, I'd been taught that it was important to earn a reputation as hardworking and easygoing. "You never know who they'll be shooting with next!" my agent would remind me. We finished our meal relatively quickly, and I helped bring dishes to the sink as Jonathan washed them. "Thank you, that was so good," I said politely. I turned and leaned against the counter, opening my phone. Jonathan sneered. "You girls and your Instagram. You're obsessed! I don't get it," he said, shaking his head and drying a plate with a dish towel.

The makeup artist painted on a bright-red lipstick, and I changed into a high-waisted pink lingerie set. We headed to the upstairs bedroom to begin shooting. I sat up on an antique brass bed frame, my knees pressing into the faded floral-print sheets. As Jonathan shot the first Polaroid, I explained that modeling was just about making money for me. "When the economy crashed and I started to get more opportunities to work, it just made sense that I'd pursue this while I could," I said. I was used to defining myself with this explanation, to men especially. "I'm not dumb; I know modeling has its expiration date. I just want to save a lot of money and then go back to school or start making art or whatever."

Jonathan frowned as he inspected the Polaroid. "You girls always end up spending too much money on shoes and bags," he said. "It's not a way to save real money."

"I don't buy bags," I said weakly, but I began to doubt myself. I was dumbfounded by his easy dismissal of my life's plan, and began to panic. *What if he was right? What if at the end of this I really would have nothing?*

He paused then and turned, silently walking back downstairs to the kitchen. I followed behind, shoeless and in my lingerie set. He spread the Polaroids out on the table and scratched his head, inspecting them. I peered at the pictures from over his shoulder. "These are just kind of . . . boring and stiff," he said with a sigh. "Maybe take off the red lipstick, fuck up your hair." He waved his hand at the makeup artist and went to the counter to open another bottle of wine, pouring fresh glasses for himself and me. The makeup artist rubbed her nails roughly into my scalp, loosening my curls. I could feel the acidic burn of alcohol in my chest as we proceeded back upstairs.

He was turned away from me when he said, "Let's try naked now."

I'd been shot nude a handful of times before, always

by men. I'd been told by plenty of photographers and agents that my body was one of the things that made me stand out among my peers. My body felt like a superpower. I was confident naked—unafraid and proud. Still, though, the second I dropped my clothes, a part of me dissociated. I began to float outside of myself, watching as I climbed back onto the bed. I arched my back and pursed my lips, fixating on the idea of how I might look through his camera lens. Its flash was so bright and I'd had so much wine that giant black spots were expanding and floating in front of my eyes.

"*iCarly*," Jonathan said, smirking as he shot. Only his mouth was visible, the rest of his face eclipsed by his camera. That was the name of the Nickelodeon show I'd been on for two episodes while in high school.

I put my lingerie back on, and we made our way back downstairs, Jonathan in front of me, gripping the Polaroids in his fists before dropping them on the kitchen table. My face was hot from the wine, and my cheeks glowed and throbbed. He was excited as he scrutinized the pictures, holding one up close to his face and then letting it fall again.

"You know, I thought you would be bigger. A big girl," he said, his brow furrowing as he picked up another Polaroid for inspection. He told me that when he googled me prior to our meeting, he'd seen a particular shoot that left him with this impression.

"You know, big-boned. Fat." He half smiled.

"Yeah, no," I said, laughing. "I'm like really, really tiny."

I knew what pictures he was referencing, from early in my career. I hated them, and I hated the way I'd felt while shooting them. I hated the way the stylist had made comments about my body, about how I could never be a fashion model. I also knew, even though I never would have admitted it, that I'd been less concerned with my weight at the time of that shoot. Freer. I enjoyed food more and didn't think so much about the shape of my ass. I didn't have to; I wasn't relying on modeling as much then.

I sipped my wine. "What should we shoot next?"

Time warped in the glow of the warm yellow lamps of Jonathan's living room, the vintage lingerie draped over the musty, floral-printed armchairs. As the night went on, I became sweaty and exhausted and bleary-eyed. But I was still determined. I liked to check out the first few Polaroids Jonathan took with each new "look" and adjust my pose and body accordingly before we continued. I could feel him bristle as I exclaimed, "Oh, I like that one!"

"This one, though," he said, holding the stack of Polaroids to his chest and flicking one around so I could catch a quick glance of it. "This one is so good because of your nipples. Your nipples change so much from hard to soft. But I like them when they're gigantic," he said, opening his phone to show me a vintage pinup of a woman with oversize nipples. "I love when they're giant," he told me. "Giant and exaggerated." He looked back to his phone, and the corners of his mouth turned up slightly. I said nothing and nodded, confused but somehow feeling that he meant to insult me. I felt my stomach turn.

I had no sense of what time it was when the makeup artist announced she was going to bed. I can't remember if we had stopped shooting and were just looking at the pictures together or what. I'm sure she was sick of my posturing with Jonathan. I remember the way she sighed as she turned away from me, vanishing. I stiffened as her presence dissolved from the living room. I was upset with her for leaving me, but I didn't want to admit to myself that her presence had made a difference. *I can handle him alone*, I thought. *She was a buzzkill anyway.* I sat up, erect. I started talking faster and louder. I was pumped full of so much sugary wine that I felt wide awake, albeit very, very drunk.

The next thing I remember is being in the dark.

The yellow lights were switched off, and I was cold, shivering, and huddled under a blanket. Jonathan and I were on his couch, and the rough texture of his jeans rubbed against my bare legs. He was asking me about my boyfriends. My mouth was chalky, but I remember I was still talking a lot—about my dating history, which guys I really loved, which ones were whatever. As I spoke, I absentmindedly rubbed my feet against one another and against his for warmth. He told me he liked "that foot thing you're doing," and I remember this moment more clearly than anything else. I hate that Jonathan commented on something I've done throughout my life to comfort myself. I hate that sometimes, even now, when I rub my feet together because I'm cold or afraid or exhausted, I think of Jonathan.

Most of what came next was a blur except for the feeling. I don't remember kissing, but I do remember his fingers suddenly being inside of me. Harder and harder and pushing and pushing like no one had touched me before or has touched me since. I could feel the shape of myself and my ridges, and it really, really hurt. I brought my hand instinctively to his wrist and pulled his fingers out of me with force. I didn't say a word. He stood up abruptly and scurried silently into the darkness up the stairs.

I touched my forehead with the coolness of my palm and breathed in through my nose. I felt the bristled texture of the old couch against my back. My body was sore and fragile, and I kept stroking parts of myself with the back of my hand—my arms, my stomach, my hips—maybe to calm them or maybe to make sure they were still there, attached to the rest of me. An intense headache began to beat into my temples, and my mouth was so dry I could barely close it.

I stood up carefully, pressing my bare feet against the floorboards. I climbed up the wooden stairs and into the room where we'd shot at the beginning of the night, then lay down on the thin flowery sheets.

I shivered uncontrollably. I was both confused as to why Jonathan had left without a word and terrified that he would come back. I listened for a sign of him as I watched the blue light of dawn peek in through the window. I thought about Jonathan's daughter. *Does she normally sleep in this bed?* I wondered.

Later in the morning, I woke with a vicious hangover. I dressed quickly in the clothes I'd been wearing the day before and noticed that my hands were shaking. Downstairs, Jonathan was making coffee, and the makeup artist was already up and dressed and sitting hunched over a mug. Jonathan didn't react much to my arrival. "You want coffee?" he asked. My temples pounded. "Sure," I half-heartedly chimed, opening Instagram. Jonathan had put up one of the Polaroids from the night before.

He had captioned it simply "*iCarly.*"

It was only as I sat on the bus headed back to the city that I realized Jonathan had never paid me back for the fare.

A FEW MONTHS later, my agent received the oversize, heavy magazine with the Polaroids printed in its pages. Of the hundreds we had shot, only a handful were included, mostly black-and-white ones.

A couple were favorites I'd pointed out to Jonathan on the night of the shoot. I was relieved to see that he'd done a tasteful edit, and I went so far as to think he might have chosen the images he remembered I liked. Years passed, and I tucked the images and Jonathan somewhere deep in my memory. I never told anyone about what happened, and I tried not to think about it.

A few years after my photo shoot, I received a call from a well-known magazine asking if they could help promote my new book of photographs.

"What book?"

By then, I'd appeared in David Fincher's *Gone Girl* and on the covers of international magazines. When the news broke of a book being sold with my name on it—the cover was completely white and read only "EMILY RATAJKOWSKI," in bold black lettering— several media outlets reached out to me directly, thinking they were being generous by offering their support to a new project of mine.

Confused, I searched my name online. There it was: *Emily Ratajkowski*, the book, priced at $80. Some of the images were posted on Jonathan's Instagram, and they were among the most revealing and vulgar Polaroids he had taken of me.

I was livid and frantic. New articles about the book, accompanied by images, were popping up hourly. My fingers went numb as I read the comments from eager customers on Jonathan's page. His followers were skyrocketing, as were the followers of @imperialpublishing, a "publishing company"—I realized after just a few moments of research—that Jonathan had personally funded and set up solely for the purpose of making this book.

I wondered what kind of damage this would do to my career as an actor. Everyone had told me to shy away from being "sexy" in order to be taken seriously, and now an entire book containing hundreds of images of me, some of them the most compromising and sexual photos of me ever taken, was available for purchase. And from what was being said online, a lot of people believed the entire situation had been my doing. I, after all, had posed for the photos.

My lawyer sent cease and desist letters: one to Jonathan's makeshift publishing company and one to a gallery on the Lower East Side that had announced it would be holding an exhibition of the Polaroids. My lawyer argued that Jonathan had no right to use the images beyond their agreed-upon usage. When I agreed to shoot with Jonathan, I had consented only for the photos to be printed in the magazine they were intended for. The gallery responded by going to the *New York Times* and telling the paper that it had a signed model release from me. By that time, I'd stopped working with my agent, who'd quit the industry, but reading this, I called her in a panic.

"I never signed anything. Did you?" I asked, trying to catch my breath. It's fairly typical for agents to sign releases on behalf of models (a pretty unacceptable norm), but I knew she wasn't sloppy. Then again, she was the one who'd sent me to Jonathan's home. I felt suddenly terrified. If I hadn't been protected during my shoot with Jonathan, what did that mean for all the other thousands, maybe millions, of photos of me that had been taken over the years? I began to run through the countless shoots I'd done in my early career. It had been only two years since the 4chan hacking. I found myself touching the place on my scalp where my hair had fallen out.

"I'll check my old email server," she promised. "But I am almost a hundred percent sure I didn't sign anything."

The next day, she forwarded me an email sent in the days following the shoot, in which the agency had requested Jonathan's signature on the model release. She wrote that she hadn't found an email in response with the release signed by him. "And I didn't sign anything he sent either!!!" she wrote. There was no release.

When my lawyer called the *New York Times* to let the paper know that whatever documents Jonathan and the gallery were claiming to have did not exist, he was informed that Jonathan had "supplied a copy of the release" signed by my former agent. I was shocked. My lawyer and I got on the phone the next day with the agent, who was sure she hadn't signed it. "It must have been forged," my lawyer announced. I felt my frustration grow. I knew I had never signed anything; I had never agreed to anything. No one had asked me.

"What can I do?" I asked again, but in a smaller

voice. I was still holding on to a faith in our system, a system I had thought was designed to protect people from these kinds of situations.

The problem with justice, or even the pursuit of justice, in the US is that it costs. A lot. For the four days of letters and calls for which I had enlisted my lawyer's services, I'd racked up a bill of nearly $8,000. And while I did have fame, I didn't have the kind of money I'd told Jonathan I hoped to have one day. I'd heard from friends that Jonathan was a rich kid who had never needed a paycheck in his life. My dad was a high school teacher; my mom was an English teacher. I had no one in my life to swoop in and help cover the costs.

The next day, my lawyer informed me, on yet another billable call, that pursuing the lawsuit, expenses aside, would be fruitless. Even if we did "win" in court, all it would mean was that I'd come into possession of the books and maybe, if I was lucky, be able to ask for a percentage of the profits.

"And the pictures are already out there now. The internet is the internet," he said to me matter-of-factly.

I watched as *Emily Ratajkowski* sold out and was reprinted once, twice, and then three times. "Reprint coming soon," Jonathan announced on his Instagram. I tweeted about what a violation this book was, how he was using and abusing my image for profit without my consent. In bed alone, I used my thumb to scroll through the replies.

They were unrelenting.

"Using and abusing? This is only a case of a celebrity looking to get more attention. This is exactly what she wants."

"You could always keep your clothes on and then you won't be bothered by these things," a woman wrote.

"I'm not sure why she would want to stop her fans from viewing these Polaroids," Jonathan said in an interview. I had a desire to disappear, to fade away. My insides ached. I developed a new habit of sleeping during the day.

The gallery on the Lower East Side held an opening for the exhibition of Jonathan's pictures of me, and I looked up photos from the event online. My name was written on the wall in black lettering. The place was so packed they had to leave the door open and let the crowd pour out onto the sidewalk. I saw photos of men in profile, gripping beers and wearing hipster jackets, standing inches from my naked photos, their postures slumped and their silly fedoras cocked back as they absorbed the neatly framed images. I couldn't believe how many people had turned up despite my very public protest. Speaking out about the images had only drawn more attention to the show, the book, and to Jonathan. I blocked everyone on Instagram who was involved, but I didn't let myself cry. When anyone mentioned the book or the show to me, I just

shook my head and said softly, "So fucked-up," like I
was talking about someone else's life. (When the fact-
checker I worked with on this essay reached out to
Jonathan about what happened that night after the
shoot, he said my allegations were "too tawdry and
childish to respond to." He added: "You do know who
we are talking about right? This is the girl that was
naked in *Treats!* magazine, and bounced around naked
in the Robin Thicke video at that time. You really want
someone to believe she was a victim?")

Years passed, and Jonathan released a second book
of my images, then a third. He had another show at
the same gallery. I looked him up online occasionally;
I almost felt like I was checking in on a part of me,
the part of me he now owned. For years, while I built
a career, he'd kept that Emily in the drawers of his
creaky old house, waiting to whore her out. It was
intoxicating to see what he'd done with this part of me
he'd stolen.

I found an extensive new interview with him, and
my chest tightened when I saw the headline: "Jonathan Leder Reveals Details of His Emily Ratajkowski
Shoot (NSFW)." The article began with his description
of how we'd come to shoot together. He managed to
make himself sound like a sought-after photographer
and me some random model who had been desperate
to shoot with him. "I had worked with over 500 models by that point in my career," he said. "And I can tell

you that Emily Ratajkowski . . . was one of the most comfortable models I had ever worked with in terms of her body. She was neither shy or self-conscious in any way. To say she enjoyed being naked is an understatement. I don't know if it empowered her or she enjoyed the attention."

I felt dizzy as I wondered the same thing. What does true empowerment even feel like? Is it feeling wanted? Is it commanding someone's attention? "We had a lot of discussions about music, art, the industry, and the creative process," Jonathan said in the interview. "She was very pleasant to speak with, and very intelligent and well-spoken, and cultured. That, more than anything, in my opinion, set her apart from so many other models." I felt myself on the carpet of Jonathan's living room, the texture of it rubbing into my skin as I posed and talked about art-making, and felt a deep twinge of shame. I promised myself that I wouldn't look him up anymore.

At the end of 2020, Jonathan published yet another book of the photos, this one hardbound. I've often stood in my kitchen and stared at myself in the large Richard Prince piece, contemplating whether I should sell it and use the money to sue. I could try to force him to cease production of his books; I could tangle him up in a legal fight that drains us both, but I'm not convinced that spending any more of my resources on Jonathan would be money well spent. Eventually,

Jonathan will run out of "unseen" crusty Polaroids, but I will remain as the real Emily; the Emily who owns the high-art Emily, and the one who wrote this essay, too. She will continue to carve out control where she can find it.

# Pamela

---

S WAS LATE, as usual.

In our first month of dating, S had announced that he was going to make sure I always knew where he was. He'd held his iPhone in his palm, screen facing outward so I could see it. He pressed on my contact and, with an intentional and animated tap of his finger, hit "Share location."

"See," he'd said. "No secrets."

From then on, whenever I opened the map on my phone, S's picture would appear in a small icon on the screen.

This gesture had surprised me. Of all the things I wanted to know about S, his exact location at any given moment was fairly low on the list. Still, I'd taken it as an offering, a sign of his willingness to *share* in a more general sense: his life, his emotions, his experiences.

Nearly three years later, I'd often find myself using his shared location to figure out when he'd *actually* arrive to meet me, since his own estimates were usually off.

S was born and raised in New York and inexperienced at navigating the freeways and traffic patterns of LA.

"Just don't bother trying to go anywhere anytime between three thirty p.m. and eight p.m., okay?" I'd explained.

"Okay," he'd said, putting on his sunglasses and giving me a quick kiss. "I'll text you when I'm finishing up my day." S always seemed spread too thin when we were in LA. There were too many meetings, too many phone calls, too much traffic.

It was silly, really, that he was coming back home to the Eastside of Los Angeles from the Westside, since the party was on the Westside and we were already late. I checked S's location. He was going to be at least another hour, and after texting him, "you're going to be super fucking late," I resolved to take my time getting ready. I poured a large glass of red wine, showered, and wrapped my hair in a towel. I added big fat wings of eyeliner to the corners of my eyes, lined my mouth with a deep mauve, applied extra-gooey lip gloss to my lips, and slipped on a black strapless tube dress that clung to my ass with purpose.

I wanted to wear a boot or something casual as a shoe, since this party was hosted by S's agency, not mine. I didn't like the idea of appearing too dressed up or too sexy in a crowd of people who, I knew, would treat me like arm candy no matter what I wore. But I couldn't find a shoe that looked right with the hemline of the tube dress, so I gave up and put on heels with straps that crisscrossed up my ankles and calves. They hurt, but these, I decided after texting pictures to a few friends, were my best option.

Once I finished inspecting myself in the mirror, I took the heels off and lay down on our bed. I knew the outfit was sexier than I'd planned on, but it felt like some kind of insurance at this film-industry party. Dressing up and performing the role that everyone expected from me was comfortable. *Beautiful girl should show up looking beautiful, right?* I thought. *Worse than arm candy is being invisible, right? Right?* Nicki Minaj blasted from my phone. "Got a bow on my panties because my ass is a present," she sang.

*Now that I'm ready, might as well take a couple of selfies.* I tilted my chin down, held up my phone, and checked myself on the screen as I clicked away. A text from S appeared at the top of my reflection: "15 minutes baby! Traffic was insane."

I ignored him with a swipe of my finger. I selected one of the selfies, posting it on Instagram. "All dressed up, no place to go," I typed, and threw my phone down

next to me. I stared at the ceiling while Nicki continued to rap.

S arrived a few minutes later, all crinkled laugh lines
and warmth. I eyed him, annoyed, as he climbed onto
the bed next to me. "You're an hour and a half late,
asshole. It's rude." We'd had this conversation countless
times before, and I was worn down by it. *Who cares,
anyway? I had a nice time getting ready*, I thought.
Besides, here he was, better late than never, smelling
like the best kind of sweat and smiling at me, ready to
love me up. What was the point of making a big deal
of this right before a party where we'd be surrounded
by hundreds of people? I wanted us to feel connected
and maybe even have some fun, for fuck's sake. *Let it
go*, I told myself.

"I'm sorry, seriously, okay? I got the timing wrong.
But I'm here now and I wanted to come home to see
you and . . . have some time," S said, pulling up my
dress without taking his eyes off my face. He kissed
my nose, and I giggled and then frowned. "Rude!" I
said, and S laughed and began edging his way down
my body.

"I'm so happy to see you," he said, and he sounded
so genuine I couldn't help but feel a wave of love wash
over me.

Later, S lay on my stomach and I wrapped my arms
around his head, watching his curly hair rise and fall
with my breathing. Eventually he got up and went to

the bathroom, and I strapped my heels back on. As we headed out the door, switching off the lights and setting the alarm, I threw on a brown leather trench over my dress. "I just don't want to be cold," I told myself.

The party S's agency was hosting was at a big fancy house owned by a former Beatle. Early on in our relationship, I'd told S that I hated parties like this. And he told me he hated agents. "They're talentless and do nothing and ugh . . . just the worst." Still, I struggled to understand his attitude to the film industry. I'd watch him take calls with his wireless headphones, laughing and sucking on his Juul, and I'd wonder: Had he been seduced by Hollywood or was he just working the system to succeed? The voice he used for these work calls was unfamiliar to me; even his laugh was different. The idea that he might actually *enjoy* the boys' club of agents, producers, and actors bothered me. I was surprised at how repelled I felt watching him work sometimes. *Or is this just him being good at his job?* I wasn't sure.

On the cab ride over, I felt uneasy. "Hey," I said to S. "Don't leave me tonight. Like, obviously, we can go have our various conversations, blah blah. But just, like, when we're walking around? You know?" I put my hand on his knee.

"Okay, sure," S replied, giving me a kiss on the lips. "No problem." He looked handsome, dressed down in a crew-neck sweatshirt and black Timbs, the hair on his face at just the right length to accentuate his strong jawline.

One night years ago, before S and I had started seeing each other romantically, he met me and a group of my friends at a hotel party. "Come by and hang," I remember texting him. It was all casual, but I knew how much I liked him the second he walked in the door. He was wearing black Timbs then, too, the same ones he wore to the courthouse when we got married.

I'd been drinking a lot that night and feeling light and fizzy in a good way. Even though we didn't look at each other much, I always knew where S was in the room. I could feel his attention on me, even when I stole a quick glance and found him looking straight ahead, talking to someone else. I was shaking my hips to the music, knowing S was watching, when a guy came up and asked to take a photo with me. "Sure!" I said, bending over to put my drink down. He was thin and had an accent. I took him for a European tourist.

I never liked how guys would find ways to touch me when they took pictures with me, but I was used to it, and so I'm not sure if I even flinched when I felt this guy's fingers wrap around the other side of my bare midriff. My attitude was, *Ask them not to touch you and it makes the whole interaction last longer, so why not just get it over with?*

"Hey, no touching," I heard S say from behind us. I swiveled around to see him, leaning against a couch. He shook his finger and furrowed his brow.

"Sorry," the guy said, dropping his hands from my body instantly. I'd never been with a man who interjected himself in that way before. My boyfriend before S would never speak up when someone approached or touched me. I assumed he meant to be respectful, showing that he knew I could handle these kinds of situations on my own, which I'd always thought I appreciated. In that moment, though, watching S, all relaxed yet assertive, telling this guy to back the fuck off, I thought, *Wow, well, this is nice.*

In the years since, we'd gotten together and our careers had changed. The movie S had recently produced had been well received by critics and performed well at the box office. People wrote articles about Oscar buzz and, when the film was snubbed, important directors S admired tweeted angrily about the "injustice of the Academy." When paparazzi pictures of us were published now, they described S as "a successful producer" and even sometimes linked to a trailer for his movie. It was everything S had been working toward for over ten years, and I was proud of him.

I, on the other hand, had decided to stop being an actor, at least for the time being. I'd auditioned for just two roles in two years, a tiny fraction of the number of auditions I'd been doing when we started seeing each other. "I only want to do projects that I can produce or be a part of on a creative level," I told everyone, which was true, but it was also true was that I no longer knew what the fuck I wanted from Hollywood.

No one in the industry knew why I'd stopped acting, and most assumed it wasn't by choice. Actors and
models couldn't possibly want something else, they
figured. Every woman wants to be rich and famous
for being desirable. I couldn't fault them for thinking
that way. Hell, I'd thought that way for most of my
twenties.

Despite my better judgment, it bothered me that
the people at this party would look at me as a failure
or nothing more than a piece of ass. Even though I
thought they were assholes, it frustrated me that I'd
lost their respect. On a good day, I'd call people sexist
who condemned a woman for capitalizing on her body.
On a bad day, I'd hate myself and my body, and every
decision I'd made in my life seemed like a glaring mistake. Mostly, though, I knew I was a whole, complex
person with thoughts and ideas and things I wanted to
make and say. I wanted so desperately to prove them
all wrong. I just hadn't gotten the chance yet.

I liked being in control, and I'd learned that an
actor's control was limited. It was also true that for
some time I'd been battling a serious depression that
was, at least partially, the result of years of making
myself digestible for the same kind of men that S now
laughed with over the phone. My own company was
growing, and my modeling work continued to pay the
bills. I'd started therapy twice a week and had begun
to think of myself as a writer. I knew fame was not all
I had imagined it would be—it certainly didn't make

me feel powerful in the way I'd thought it would. It wasn't clear what Hollywood could offer that would make me feel fulfilled and, simply, happy. I wanted to remove myself from this world in some way, but it was the world in which my husband was just beginning to find his footing.

So here I was, miserable but trying to put my best face on to play the role of supportive wife. I desperately wished that S and I could laugh together at all the bullshit the party represented, but I knew we weren't completely aligned.

We pulled up to the ex-Beatle's house and entered the glossy marble foyer. Models I knew strutted by in sparkly mesh dresses and five-inch stilettos, smiling and waving to say hello, their hair and makeup professionally done. S and I held hands as we pushed farther into the party; he kept his right hand free and extended it to the countless men in suits who greeted him with variations on "What up, man?" and "Hey, congrats, man." I smiled. My complicated relationship to the industry aside, I felt a sense of pride as S moved through a roomful of people who, two years ago, would not have acknowledged him in the same way. It must have felt good. He'd committed years of his life to this film—weekends and nights and long days. Watching him throughout that process had taught me something about patience and working hard.

S led us to a corner where his partners and some other friends were standing together. I kept my coat on and secured with a tight knot around my waist, my tube dress covered up. I positioned myself against a tall stool, my feet already hurting, and dropped in and out of a conversation S was having with an indie musician, taking sips of my watered-down tequila soda and tasting chunks of lime. I could feel a headache coming on. *Shouldn't have worn these shoes*, I thought. Then, *What's one more night in heels? You've done it before and you'll do it again.*

S, focused on his conversation, wasn't looking at me much. The music was loud, making it nearly impossible to hear anything without someone coming up very close to your face. I watched the musician lean into S's ear, nodding and gesturing. How lame I must seem to him, I thought, half sitting on a stool with nothing to say. *Playing into exactly what he expects from the model wife*, I thought. *I shouldn't have come.*

*　*　*

Three hours had passed. I'd taken quite a few selfies and had enough polite, forced conversations to last me a lifetime.

"So what are you working on?" they'd ask, smiling.

"I'm trying to write a book, actually," I'd say.

"What?" They'd bring their ear close to my mouth and squint, trying to focus.

"A book," I'd repeat. "I'm writing a book." And they'd pull back to search my face, thinking before they spoke again.

"Like, by yourself? You're writing it?"

"Yeah!" I'd shrug as if to say, *Crazy, right? Little ol' me! Go figure.*

"Well, that's . . . cool." Then an exclamation of relief: "Oh, I *love* what you're doing with the bikinis! Seems like you guys are killing it!"

"Thank you so much," I'd say, bending my head forward in a tiny bow. "Really means a lot."

"I'm going to do a lap." One of us would bring the exchange to an end, and I'd wander off, only to have a similar conversation with someone else.

I was tired. On the dance floor, a few men in white button-down shirts and loosened ties stuck out their arms and moved from side to side, watching their partners wiggle in circles. I wasn't drunk enough for that. Besides, I didn't want to have to take off my coat and I could feel my feet swelling against the leather straps of my shoes. S was between conversations.

I approached him. "How you doing?" I said. "You know, we've been here for a while now and it's almost one." I looked around the room as if observing it for the first time. "It's definitely clearing out," I said.

"Okay, okay." He was drunk, I could tell. "Can we go say hi to Miley and her manager? He said we should find them before we leave."

I sighed.

"They're just over there," S said, his voice rising, as he pointed across the room. "Come on."

Most of the familiar faces had left, and the room

felt sloppy and warped in the way rooms do when everyone in them has gotten drunk on hard liquor. I sensed men's eyes on me as we moved through the crowd. "Sorry," I said as we pushed through. "Excuse me." I kept my head down.

When S spotted Miley, his hand slipped from mine and he went a few paces ahead. With my aching feet, I couldn't keep up with him, or maybe I didn't want to. In that moment, two warm, clammy hands attached to my back.

"Emma!"

I swiveled round to see a man with thick black eyebrows standing to my left. On my right was a blond man's eager, sweaty face. I was surrounded. Another person bumped into me. Cool liquid spilled onto my bare toes.

"Can we get a photo?" the blond man asked, already extending his digital camera. "Sure," I said as the flash went off and I tried to sneak in a quick, polite smile.

"Thanks, Emma!" he said. S was maybe ten feet away now, talking, grinning widely, his hands animated. I fumed, exhausted and angry with my head and feet throbbing. *I'm not going to chase after him*, I decided, and headed to the other side of the bar, where I'd spotted a friend of S's who'd worked on his movie.

"Hi, Nate," I greeted him, imagining S looking around for me. *Fuck him*, I thought. *He can come find me.*

A few minutes had passed when I felt S's hand on

my elbow. I spun around, my eyes hard. Something swelled inside me. I felt as if I could either smack him or start sobbing.

"Where'd you go?" he asked, annoyed.

"*You*," I emphasized, "left me. I didn't *go* anywhere."

He shook his head in disbelief, matching my anger with his own. He threw his hands up.

"Just stop it, Emily! That's not what happened." He sounded almost frantic. I breathed in the hot air and gritted my teeth

"No. I was walking behind you and two creeps grabbed me. And you didn't fucking stop to look back and kept running over to Miley fucking Cyrus. I had to take pictures with these guys and they touched my back and I had asked you one thing. I asked you to just not fucking leave me."

"You could've told them no pictures! I was three feet away from you, Emily. Jesus fucking Christ."

"You weren't three feet away. You were on the other side of the room saying hi to Miley Cyrus."

"Yeah! And she was asking where *you* were! She wanted to say hi to *you*. *You're* her friend!" His face was red.

S took a deep breath and put his hand on my shoulder. I could tell he was trying to calm down. He started to speak, but a voice interrupted him.

"You two, can I just say—" We turned to see S's agent, Berg, holding a drink, his eyes heavy with alcohol.

I'd never seen Berg without a suit and didn't know him very well, but I'd spent enough time in his company to have developed a dislike for him. He'd talk over me, looking only at S. Sometimes I'd tell myself I was just being a bitch, that Berg was focused on S because he was his client. Other times, I thought he didn't particularly like women. At the least, I was sure he didn't think much of me. Once, he'd told me I should "be grateful for my fame while it lasts."

A few months before, at a different party, Berg came up to a group of people I was standing with.

"Okay, I just need to say this," he announced to the group, his eyes unfocused and looking past me. "I just said to someone, 'Don't rape me on this deal,' right?" He paused and ran a hand through his hair, his eyes shifting. "And they said, 'Can you not say that?'" He shook his head and took a sip of his drink. "This shit is getting ridiculous. *Fuck-ing* ridiculous. Like what, I can't say *rape* now?"

Now Berg stood before us, clearly drunk, looking greasy. S and I stopped our fight. I tasted my drink, trying to put my frustration aside.

"You two, let me just say," he began again. "I mean, S, I've only seen heat like this five times in my career before. Five fucking times. And it's not just heat," he paused, "because you're fucking *good*." The ice cubes clinked against the side of his glass.

"Everyone knows you're famous, Emily, but I always say, S is the one, S is the one who . . ." He trailed off, taking a swig of his drink, his nose disappearing into the glass.

"Come on, Berg," I said, forcing a smile. "You think I don't know how special this guy is? I married him." I felt S's hand touch my back and I wrapped my arm around him in return. "We don't care what people say." I paused. "That's all just noise."

Berg began again. "And Emily, I mean you're really fucking famous, but—"

"She *is* really fucking famous," S said in a soft voice, almost to himself. I knew he was trying to signal that he was sorry for leaving me alone with the creepy selfie guys.

"Yeah, I mean, listen, I'm not even on social media, and I know how fucking famous she is. I'm like . . ." He cocked his head to one side. "She's like Pamela Anderson before the hep C."

My body stiffened and my chest tightened as if someone had poured ice down my spine, so cold it burned. Although S didn't move an inch, I sensed him straighten up and grow larger beside me. His face was blank, flat, the lines of warmth around his eyes gone in an instant.

"You need to shut the fuck up now," he said, his voice stern and his body still. This was the kind of thing he'd said countless times before to Berg, on calls when they were joking around, but now his face was frozen and Berg wasn't laughing.

I wanted to say, *You're a sexist piece of shit, Berg.*

Pamela Anderson was an actor with a sex tape that had been stolen from her home and distributed against her will. Hollywood didn't take her seriously. The industry had used her as a sex object and then turned her into a joke, an insult directed at other women. Pamela represented the idea that women have an expiration date on their usability. And the hep C? Was my fate so clear?

I wanted to make this dweeb of a man feel like the tiny, insignificant person he was. I wanted to say, *You don't know me at all, you've never tried to know me, and the fact that you think my fame and status as a desirable woman are all I have to offer says more about you than it does about me.* But this was S's night, and this was the agent who'd been working with him since the beginning of his career. Their relationship dated back further than our marriage. S talked to him nearly every day. That very morning, I'd heard them discussing a dream deal with HBO that Berg was facilitating. In that way, Berg was a powerful, important man.

I was filled with resentment at S for making me come to the party, for putting me in this position. I wanted to scream at him, *I am past this! I am better than this!* I thought about the way that S had glided through the room, a room full of men who only two years before had been kissing Harvey Weinstein's ring and encouraging their young female clients to take meetings with him in hotel rooms. I hated that my husband was at all connected to these men, and I hated that I couldn't scream in Berg's face on account of him. I hated myself for trying to look beautiful. But more than anything, I resented S for making me need him.

"No? Too far?" Berg said quickly, his eyes shifting between us. I could hear Berg talking, but his voice and the sounds of the party fell into a dull, blank space.

I pulled my coat tighter around my body and slid over to Nate, sitting a few feet down from me, tucking myself next to him. I caught his eye as he laughed, mid-conversation. He studied my face. "You okay?" he asked.

The words poured out of me. "Berg is drunk and he just said, 'You're like Pamela Anderson before the hep C,' and I don't know what to do and S is still over there with him."

I wanted Nate to tell me what to do, to tell me I should disappear, to give me permission to be outraged. Anything.

"I'm searching for how he might've meant that in a good way and I have to admit, I'm coming up with nothing," Nate offered. "I'm sorry he said that to you. He's an idiot, anyway."

S appeared in front of me then, not looking at me, as he talked to yet some other man, his mind somewhere else.

"Can we please go now?" I asked in a small voice.

Cars lined the street outside as we stood under an awning, rain tapping against the fabric. I called an Uber. When we stepped out into the rain to climb into the car, the white flashes of the paparazzi's cameras nearly blinded us. I kept my eyes on my feet, praying I wouldn't slip in my stilettos against the wet concrete. S slammed the door shut, the world suddenly quiet. A pap ran to the front of the car, a red baseball hat backward on his head, his camera held up, flashing away through the front window into the backseat.

"Jesus Christ," S said. The car could barely move in the traffic. My eyes burned with tears. I hated myself for crying, and that was when the tears really started, unrelentingly and uncontrollably.

The car crawled forward; I heard the driver signal a turn. *Tick, tick, tick.* The bright pops of light were gone. We were silent for a moment. "Well, that was . . ." S paused. "Listen, I am so sorry he said that to you. That was awful."

"*I'm* so sorry," I cried. "I'm so embarrassed." S put his arm around me, but nothing felt right. I didn't want S to apologize for Berg; I wanted him to say how much he hated everything Berg stood for. I wanted him to pick a side, but I knew that wasn't fair; it wasn't so simple. I cried harder.

"You shouldn't be sorry! God, no," he said. I lay down in his lap, my face away from him, buried in his thighs.

"I just . . . It all would have been okay if I just wasn't there," I said. "It all would have been normal. You could've had a good time." I shuddered. I thought about my stupid selfies, my stupid dress, and my stupid eyeliner. I shut my eyes tight. I felt a sudden urge to disappear. I imagined being able to breathe in so deeply that my body would dissolve into the air I'd sucked in, and then I'd no longer be in my body, in my physical self, in this car with S, or anywhere at all. *You are the problem*, I thought to myself. *Something is wrong with you. And if you were taken out of the equation, everything would be just fine.*

# Men Like You

---

██████████

I would like to present a great opportunity for Emily's consideration.

There is a lot of interest from the NFT / Crypto world around treats!, in particular the incredible images Emily and I shot together for her first ever cover ████████████████████ ████████████████████████████████████████ ████████████████████████████████████████ ████████ give the opportunity for Emily to tell a story of empowerment people would love to hear.

████████████████████████████████████████ ██████████████ Emily's first ever Instagram post was her and I holding the cover ██████████████ we really didn't know how powerful social media would be.

 Emily has gone on to accomplish so many amazing things, including motherhood

this could be huge, along with the story that helped start a career.

Steve[1]

Hi Steve,

Here is one of my favorite quotes from an interview you gave to InsideHook (whatever that is) in 2016, where you talk about our first meeting:

So she sat there for about an hour, and no one paid any attention to her. And she had this shitty portfolio. The girl was modeling lingerie for Frederick's of Hollywood's e-commerce website. I mean, the

---

[1] This is a redacted email sent to my former manager in 2020.

worst stuff. The girl could hardly get a job. She was 5'4" with these huge tits. Tony suggested I send her home, so I went up to her and said, 'Look, sorry. You've got to go,' and she went, 'Oh, okay.' And then for some weird reason I started talking to her, and she was actually a really smart girl.

I well remember the day you describe. I had just dropped out of college and hadn't yet found a new place to live in Los Angeles, so I drove two and a half hours from San Diego to come and meet you. It was a Saturday. I'd already been in Los Angeles twice that week, shooting the regular catalog jobs that paid my bills. I didn't feel like making the commute again, but I understood that it was important for me to try and build my portfolio with more "tears," the pages taken from magazine editorials. I left early in the morning, drinking coffee and blasting talk radio to help me stay awake on the highway. When I arrived, the marine layer still hadn't burned off yet.

I drove back and forth on La Brea in front of your photo studio, searching for parking. I was so worried about being late and seeming unprofessional that I eventually pulled into the McDonald's lot next door and parked, praying I wouldn't get a ticket or be towed, neither of which I could afford at the time. I put on the heels I'd thrown in the backseat and grabbed my book of modeling pictures. My agent had told me to wear no makeup, but as I checked my reflection in the rearview mirror, I sneaked a tiny bit of concealer under my eyes. I wanted to appear fresh and naturally beautiful to you.

You described me as "scruffy" to the *Sun* in 2017:

> She came in wearing a black baggy smock dress with horrible four inch black plastic shoes on. It was like a bin liner and hid everything. She was sat waiting to see Tony Duran, the photographer, and he told me to send her home.

You say that you started talking to me "for some weird reason," but our conversation was no accident. Although you were nearly fifty, about thirty years my senior, I read you in an instant. I knew what I needed to do; I've had to impress men like you my entire life and be grateful for any scrap of attention. I was still a teenager, but knowing how to get noticed by people in your position was already second nature. I approached you, played it cool, and complimented you on your massive *Blow-Up* poster.

"I love that film," I said. It was true. I'd been introduced to it at the summer arts program I'd done in San Francisco in my junior year of high school, when I was smoking pot and sitting around my dorm room, toying with the idea of becoming an artist, someone who might make a movie one day rather than get naked in one. My professor had shown us *Blow-Up* for the filmmaking, but I'd been struck by the women in the film;

by their beauty and desirability and glamour. Their desperation to be seen through the lens of the blasé photographer made perfect sense to me. I had the same poster, albeit smaller, waiting to be framed and hung whenever I found a place to live.

"Really?" you asked in your British accent, as you turned to face me.

Men never notice the overcalculating that women do. They think things happen "for some weird reason" while women sing songs and do backbends and dance elaborate moves to *make* those things happen.

You started talking about your career. You told me you used to shoot for *Playboy* and that your new magazine, while full of nude girls, was "nothing like it."

You got excited when I said I'd been an art major. How surprising it must have been for you to discover that I was, to use your words, "actually a really smart girl." A mere mention of a pretentious film—it was so easy to subvert your expectations.

I wonder how many women you've disregarded in your life, written off, because you assumed they had nothing to offer beyond the way they looked. How quickly they learned that the stuff in their heads was of less value than the shape of their bodies. I bet they were all smarter than you.

You took out heavy, oversized books of vintage erotic photographs. You said they were the inspiration for your magazine. Maybe you were insecure about being a cheesy *Playboy* photographer, a Hugh Hefner

wannabe, so you jumped to prove you were an artist after I mentioned that my father was a painter. Or
maybe you were just testing me, seeing whether I really
understood the references I made. I pointed to the
pictures I liked, *ooh*ing and *aah*ing over the squeaky,
glossy pages.

I must have said something right, because you
peered up at me from the splayed pages of a Helmut
Newton book and paused to consider me, as if you
really saw me for the first time. That was when you
asked me to strip.

"Why don't you take your clothes off and put a little pair of knickers on?" You indicated the bathroom.

I acted nonchalant. "Oh, okay, sure," you remember me saying. Our memories align there. But what
you couldn't know is how deeply satisfied I was. I was
glad that our interaction had led to you wanting more
from me, happy that my commute might not have been
in vain.

I suppose that, from your perspective, this should
be the moment I thank you for. When I was younger, I
would have thought so, too. You looked past my unap-
pealing outfit and cheap shoes and figured why not,
she's not bad to talk to, let's give her a shot, see what
she's working with.

*Besides*, some part of me figured, *I love being
naked, who the fuck cares.* I'd just started to learn that
actually, *everyone* seemed to really, really care. I was
beginning to understand that I could use this attention

to my advantage. I wanted to test the waters: What is the power of my body? Is it ever *my* power?

When I came out of the bathroom topless, I stood up straight, not covering my breasts. I believed that by taking off my clothes proudly, by not letting myself be embarrassed by my nakedness, I might somehow intimidate you, shifting the dynamic. But of course there was no chance of that, when we live in a world where millions of women will jump at the chance to win the attention of men like you, Steve.

I was already an expert in assessing myself through men's eyes. I had recently started smoking cigarettes and skipping meals to maintain a tiny waist, so I felt confident that you would be impressed. I was right. When you saw my body, your eyes went wide. "Jesus fucking Christ," you said. "Where were you hiding all of *that*?"

You took my hand and walked me through the studio, past the other models, to the photographer as I stumbled, giggling, behind you in nothing but my underwear and a pair of heels. It felt so incredibly validating to be recognized by you as special.

I was nineteen. I loved driving down the coastline with the windows down, playing music. I loved the way my skin smelled after rolling in the sand when I drank too much sangria on the beach with my friends. I was eager to meet the kinds of smart, cool people I thought I'd find in LA if I was able to make enough money to move there; excited about the adult world and where I'd fit into it and what I might do. Do you remember what it was like to be nineteen?

* * *

Once, while leaving a nightclub, a famous musician plucked twenty young girls off the dance floor and had them sit in a room next to his recording studio until five in the morning. He took their phones, made them sign NDAs, and put them all together, out of the way, to wait till he was done playing his new album for some friends. Then they would all party, he said. A guy I know was there, and as he was leaving, he saw the girls crowded together. He said the room looked like the DMV.

I pictured the girls exhausted, with no internet or cameras or texts to distract themselves. A little drunk. I saw their push-up bras, their curls falling flat under the fluorescent lights.

Why do you think they waited in that room, Steve?

Maybe many years from now, maybe next week, those girls will suddenly feel upset at something and not know why. *Where is this reaction coming from?* They really won't know, they won't be able to place it, but it will be because of the way they let themselves sit in that room. The way they put on their makeup and dressed themselves up. They'll feel small and blame no one but themselves.

I so desperately craved men's validation that I accepted it even when it came wrapped in disrespect. I was those girls in that room, waiting, trading my body and measuring my self-worth in a value system that revolves around men and their desire.

*   *   *

Was I unknown when we worked together? you were asked. "Not for long," you responded. "I got all these emails from people like Kanye West and Adam Levine, who wanted to use her in campaigns. Then Robin Thicke called me."

You're right, I did get a lot of attention from well-known, powerful men. That was how I got opportunities to work, to make money and also build a career. Robin Thicke and Adam Levine hired me to be in their music videos. In the video for Maroon 5, I straddled Adam Levine in underwear as he rubbed blue paint all over my body.

The year I met you, a famous man flew me from Los Angeles to London on the promise of a job opportunity. I landed in the morning, jetlagged and sore from my narrow seat on a crowded flight. My agent had said I'd have an hour to freshen up before being taken to the man's studio, but the hotel phone rang immediately as I walked in the room to notify me that there was a car waiting. At the studio, a team of people changed my clothes and pushed me out onto a platform a few feet above where the man was sitting. His expression was unreadable as he kept his eyes on my body before I was whisked away again. I was relieved, thinking that the casting was over. I wanted to go to my hotel room and sleep, but someone came to say that the famous man wanted me to have a drink with him.

"Okay," I said, catching my reflection in the mirror. I looked exhausted. *What time was it in Los Angeles?* I wondered, afraid of the answer. "Sure."

The conversation was awkward in the backseat of his car while his friend or his assistant (in my experience, all the friends of famous men seem to be on their payroll) sat in the passenger seat. The driver stared straight ahead robotically. The man opened his laptop and lazily pressed on the keyboard as we spoke. I watched the slow-moving traffic out the window. When I glanced back, I saw that he had turned the laptop to face me. On the screen, two men and two women were having sex. The man pointed to one of the bodies.

"That one's me." He grinned, his eyes on the screen.

When I'd agreed to fly to London, my agent told me to rely on him if I needed anything. "I'm happy to be the bad guy," he'd said. As the car stopped at an upscale hotel, I shot off a quick email, without specific details, asking him to nudge his contact to release me.

We sat and ordered drinks, and just as I had with you, Steve, I did my best to present myself as more than just a body. I talked about art and music and even politics. In a way that reminded me of my meeting with you, we genuinely connected on some things.

The three of us took an elevator up to his suite. We sat in the living space for an hour or so before the assistant began to fall asleep on the couch, his eyes rolling back in his head. The famous man opened his laptop again and started to play a video I'd done for *Treats!*

"I mean, damn." he said, indicating my naked body in motion. "I can't stop watching you." *How odd*, I thought. *I'm right here in front of you.*

I checked my email for a response from my agent. "You're a big girl, Emily. Figure it out."

I mustered some courage and stood up, announcing loudly enough to wake the assistant that it was time for me to leave. As we began to walk out, the famous man stood to hug me. He pressed his body against mine and then slowly kissed my neck. We were suddenly alone; the assistant had disappeared behind the shut front door. I giggled nervously, trying to bring some levity to the vibe. "I have a boyfriend," I said, knowing that invoking another man's ownership might deter him. He breathed in my scent.

"I'll talk to you soon," I promised, smiling politely as I placed my hands on his forearms to move them off my body.

The next morning, I woke to my phone's alarm, realizing that neither my agent nor the famous man had arranged a car to take me to the airport. I found myself in the back of a cold black cab, watching the fare rise on the monitor as I silently converted pounds to dollars, hoping my credit card would clear.

The man emailed me for months. He called a few times as well, each time from a different number and always at strange times of the day and night. I stopped picking up calls from numbers I didn't recognize. Still, I was flattered by the powerful man's pursuit. I knew that if I played my cards right, making sure to distinguish myself from other women while maintaining clear boundaries, I might be able to benefit from whatever notoriety and jobs he could offer. But my heart wasn't in it. My responses were flaky and inconsistent. After I made an excuse to avoid him when he was in Los Angeles, he wrote to me: "i really wanted to Muse you and I haven't had a Muse in years smh."

*   *   *

When you visit New York City, you have likely passed by her. In Central Park, on the Manhattan Bridge, in Columbus Circle, or at the Main Branch of the New York Public Library. Perhaps you've admired the golden figure atop the Municipal Building downtown? She is everywhere: on bridges, on buildings, in parks, and in fountains. There are thirty statues of her body inside the Met alone. All these likenesses are of the same woman.

Audrey Munson was discovered by a photographer while window-shopping with her mother on Fifth Avenue. Audrey posed nude for the first time shortly thereafter, when she was still a teenager. She quickly became the model of choice for sculptors and painters of the time, all of whom obsessed over the shape of her body, over her breasts, even over the dimples on her lower back. (One sculptor warned her, "Guard those dimples, my girl. And if you ever see them going—cut out the apple pie.") In 1913, the New York *Sun* wrote: "Over a hundred artists agree that if the name of Miss Manhattan belongs to anyone in particular it is to this young woman."

Less than two decades later she attempted suicide. At the age of 40, she was committed to a psychiatric hospital. She lived out the rest of her life there, died at the age of 106, and was buried in an unmarked grave.

I suppose this is the life cycle of a muse: get discovered, be immortalized in art for which you're never paid, and die in obscurity.

Audrey herself wrote, "What becomes of the artists' models? I am wondering if many of my readers have not stood before a masterpiece of lovely sculpture or a remarkable painting of a young girl, her very abandonment of draperies accentuating rather than diminishing her modesty and purity, and asked themselves the question, 'Where is she now, this model who was so beautiful?'"

I think of her and the other naked women who line the walls and fill the halls of museums, some so ancient the color has washed from their bodies and their marble heads have fallen off. It would be easy to mistake these displays for symbols of respect, for an honor. But what were their lives? And what were their names? No one remembers.

\* \* \*

Did you think I'd never see the interviews you gave about me, Steve? Or did you think you'd never need anything more from me, so it didn't matter? Perhaps you didn't think of me at all. I suspect it was the latter.

It might surprise you that when I first read your remarks, I wasn't angry. You made them five years after we'd met. I'd just turned twenty-five. I'd become famous, and the magazine you'd sold a house to fund was failing (Had the Winklevoss twins sued you yet? Or did that come later?). But things hadn't really changed much. I was still a young woman who placed her self-worth in the hands of men like you.

I wasn't angry, because I thought you were right: My shoes *were* embarrassing. I didn't know how to dress. I'm short. I'm nothing special unless I'm naked. I should be grateful that you looked at me twice. Had you not, who knows what might have happened? As you said, "I certainly know where she would be, and it wouldn't be where she is now."

I was also ashamed. I hated myself for trying to impress you. It didn't feel as if I'd hustled you to get on in life. Instead, it felt as if I'd betrayed and fetishized myself to be appealing to you. Even the way you called me "smart" stung. I hated that I'd used the things I loved to win your attention.

I kept your interviews to myself. I was too mortified to share what'd you said with people close to me. I didn't want to run the risk that they might agree with you. I didn't want them to see me as you did.

I didn't have it in me to be angry.

Yet.

* * *

We're going to do this model search, and I want to find another twelve Emilys and make them into stars and give them an amazing platform to have a career. . . . So if I can find some girl in Russia who's picking potatoes and put her in this calendar and make her famous, that would be fantastic.

You held your casting. There is a video of it online, edited to an airy techno beat. Young women float by in bikinis, their hair flowing behind them while they arch their backs and blow kisses toward the camera you crouch behind. As each one poses, she holds a whiteboard with her name written plainly on it. Then the whiteboard is wiped clean and one young woman's name is replaced by another's.

I can't stand the thought of you using my name to recruit these girls. I hate that you point to me as an example and say, *Look at what you could have if you know how to catch my eye.*

I am angry now, not only for myself but for "some girl in Russia" and all the young women and girls who see you as a gatekeeper, who line up before you to be judged as fuckable or not.

I want to tell those girls that I'm not sure it's worth it—not the money or the attention. I'd be lying if I said that fame did not come with its gifts: Would anyone care to read what I write had I not impressed men like you?

"So let me tell you, that girl would never have had the career she has had she kept her clothes on," you say. I can see why you think that's true.

David Fincher said in an interview that when he wanted to cast a girl in *Gone Girl* whom men were obsessed with and women hated, Ben Affleck brought up my name.

Having a role in a serious film that had been cast by a well-respected director was something I was proud of. I had a fancy credit to add to my résumé, and other directors (almost always men) were impressed by my proximity to Fincher. In interviews, I knew to elaborate on how I'd worked for the role, how I'd read for the part on tape and then won it with my in-person audition with him.

But I was topless in his film. And although I had the new title of "actor," a growing bank account, and fans recognizing me on the street, I also began to get comments online that filled me with self-loathing: "this girl can't keep her clothes on"; "nice tits but not much else going on"; "enjoy your fifteen minutes before those things start to sag." The hairstylists on the set of *Gone*

*Girl* warned me that it was time to stop doing nude photoshoots now that I was no longer just a model and muse—but their guidance was confusing: Hadn't I booked the role, at least in part, because of the way I'd stripped for men like you, Steve?

\* \* \*

You'll remember when you kissed me. Or maybe you don't. We were saying goodbye after the launch party for my cover issue of your magazine. It was late, and I was drunk on sponsored champagne and how special you'd made me feel that night. You were using my body and the pictures you'd taken of it to promote your magazine, but I wasn't focused on that piece of our dynamic then. Instead I felt as if you had thrown a fancy party in my honor, with all the guests there to celebrate the most desirable girl du jour (me) in all the land (Los Angeles).

A model friend a decade older than me had called a cab to take us home. "I'll drop you off," she said. I turned to hug you and say thanks. You pushed your body against mine and softly pecked me on the lips twice, and then you pressed your mouth to mine. You slid your tongue past my teeth. I kissed you back. I thought of how you stood before the blown-up images of my naked body (they were for sale, I'd learned when I spotted the prices) telling everyone that I was a very special girl, holding a miniature bottle of Moët with one hand and circling my waist with the other.

My friend interrupted the kiss. "Come on, babe! We gotta go!" she yelled as she held the door open, waiting.

You pulled back, a glint of excitement in your eyes. You were old enough to be my father, and you knew that I shouldn't have been kissing you, but you raised an eyebrow as if you were waiting for my signal to pounce. I burst into laughter, feeling a rush of glee at the power I had in that moment as the object of your desire. My friend took me by the wrist, yanking me away from you.

"Bye, Steve," she called as she stuffed me into the car and slammed the door. I didn't resist her. The truth was that I had no interest in you, only in the way you had made me feel, in the way you'd looked at me.

"You don't want to do that," she muttered. It was dark in the backseat. I drunkenly sat next to her, still a little giddy from the kiss and slightly embarrassed by the authority she had exerted over me. I was confused. In my naïveté, I assumed that she must have been trying to control me. Now I think of her solemn profile, dimly lit, and I understand. What must she have experienced with men like you to gain the wisdom I did not yet have?

It's frightening now to think that I might have let you lay claim to my body and use it in that way as well. How much harder it would have been for me to conquer my shame at having tried to impress you, at the giddiness and gratitude I expressed, and at the way I surrendered my body to you so easily.

You say in your interview:

No one wants to see an old man fucking young girls
anymore. It's embarrassing. That may have worked
in the '70s, but women are so much more indepen-
dent and powerful these days, and that has changed.
I'm an older guy, and these girls are half my age.

You once flipped open your magazine and pointed
to a model, topless and with her mouth open, to tell me
you'd slept with her. You acted slightly sheepish about
it, although I'm not sure whether it's better or worse to
know that you understood.

*  *  *

Do you remember the triptych of my naked body? I
didn't want to do the shoot, but my agent had said it
was for breast cancer awareness and you promised it
would just be an hour of my time.

"A portion of the sales will go to some charity,"
she claimed. "And Sam Bayer is a respected, working
director. Not bad to get out in front of him."

I relented and then went to the show where the
black-and-white images of sixteen women had each
been blown up to twelve feet to line a giant room in the
art gallery. We had been sliced into threes: our heads
near the ceiling, our breasts and torsos in the center and
at eye level, our vaginas.

A few years later, I saw on Instagram that my portrait had been moved to an LA nightclub. I'd get tagged in photos of both men and women posing in front of the lower part of my body, gesturing lewdly.

* * *

You like me now that I wear nicer shoes. You're ready to call me a collaborator now that I am no longer a child, now that I have grown up and become, as you point out, a mother. (How funny that men view the life cycles of women so simply! From sex object to mother to what? Invisibility?)

The disrespect you have shown me is appalling. It is ironic that you would approach me about an NFT— something that is all about ownership and subjects being recognized and receiving their dues—when you've spent the last ten years doing anything but granting me ownership: of my career and of my images. By the way, I notice that on your Vimeo channel you now charge viewers $3.99 to watch the videos of my shoots.

* * *

I used to be unsure whether I should be grateful to you, for our friendship and the opportunities you gave me. But I'm no longer grateful. I do not believe I owe you anything. I will no longer blame myself for having become small and digestible for you. I have grown past shame and fear and into anger. It is ugly, but I am not scared of it. I want more for myself. I will proclaim all of my mistakes and contradictions, for all the women who cannot do so, for all the women we've called muses without learning their names, whose silence we mistook for consent. I stood on their shoulders to get here.

One other thing, Steve. My first post on Instagram was not a picture of you and me. My first post was on February 21, 2011, before I'd even met you. It's a photograph of my closest female friend smiling.

# Releases

In my dream I am screaming. My face is sticky with tears. A figure looms in front of me. Sometimes it's someone I am close to; other times it's someone I haven't thought about in years.

There are nights when it's no one specific, only a presence. We are always located in some place from my memories: on the street where I grew up or in an apartment I left long ago. No matter the setting, one thing is consistent: my rage. I yell. I sob. I want this person to recognize my anguish. I try and try to get their attention, but they are unresponsive and blank.

Eventually, I move to strike them, but my arms are impossibly heavy as I raise them. When a fist finally connects, there's no impact, as if I am made of nothing. There is no satisfaction and no release.

I wake from this nightmare with my heart beating hard, panic and urgency pulsing through me. I am horrified by my anger; embarrassed by its violence. What is wrong with me? Why do I have this vicious and destructive rage? I don't want to think about what might explain my distress. I tell myself that I don't deserve this degree of fury. I share my dream with no one.

Once, I asked S whether he ever dreams of fighting.

"It's awful! The worst!" I hoped he would know my frustration. "You have no impact. It's like being a ghost. Something without a body." He shrugged and reminded me that he doesn't really remember his dreams.

When I wake up from the nightmare one morning a month or so after giving birth to my son, I'm unable to shake off the intensity of feelings. I go into a virtual session with my therapist and describe it to her. She listens intently and expressively—as therapists do—before she speaks.

"In life, where does your anger go? How do you release it?"

"I don't," I say plainly.

No one likes an angry woman. She is the worst kind of villain: a witch, obnoxious and ugly and full of spite and bitterness. Shrill. I do anything to avoid that feeling, anything to stop myself from being that woman. I try to make anything resembling anger seem spunky and charming and sexy. I fold it into something small, tuck it away. I invoke my most reliable trick—I project sadness—something vulnerable and tender, something welcoming, a thing to be tended to.

My therapist peers at me, her dark framed glasses making her appear bug-eyed on my screen.

"How about you come in and break some things?" she says.

\* \* \*

In her office, I am horrified to see her holding a glass bowl filled with colorful water balloons.

"Oh no." I grimace. "I already hate this." I think about her pouring the water into the balloons for me before my arrival and shudder with humiliation. I shuffle behind her out to the roof of the building. The sun is out, but there is a chill in the air.

She places the glass bowl on the ground and stands up to face me. Only familiar with sitting across from her, I am shocked to realize for the first time that I am taller than she is. I am aware of her physicality in a way that makes me uncomfortable. I wrap my coat a little tighter, avoiding her eyes by gazing at the surrounding buildings that seem to press up against us. She walks me through the exercise.

"I've done this before myself," she offers charitably. "You have to make yourself . . . big!" She throws open her arms and spreads her legs. She widens her mouth into a large O. Her kindness makes me feel ridiculous but, more than anything, pathetic. *The level of self-involvement*, I think. *Has it really come to this?*

*I'm about to throw pink and green water balloons at a wall? Christ. I'm nearly thirty.* I am surprised to find hot tears spurting from my eyes. I laugh, embarrassed, quickly wiping one away.

"Why are you crying?" she asks.

"This is just so silly," I say, stifling a small sob.

"I don't think you're crying because this is *silly*." She crouches down to the bowl and selects a balloon. I take it, noting the fragility of its skin in my fingers.

I read once that women are more likely than men to cry when they are angry. I know that women cry out of shame. We are afraid of our anger, embarrassed by the way that it transforms us. We cry to quell what we feel, even when it's trying to tell us something, even when it has every right to exist.

I shiver, clutching at the balloon. I throw it against the wall, watching it pop with a gentle snap, and am aware of a vague sense of annoyance.

"I'm not sure this is doing much. Did the balloons have to be so colorful?" I remark. She laughs, and then hands me a small jar. "I don't think it is made of glass, so it might not break. But maybe it's better than the balloons."

I take the jar and self-consciously throw it against the wall. My arm is like a piece of limp spaghetti. I try again. The jar bounces. I imagine someone looking out their window to see a skinny woman throwing an object at a brick wall. *Pathetic*, I repeat in my head.

I think about what I must look like to the neighbors

and to my therapist. I know that embracing anger means relinquishing that control, that assessment, that distance from myself, but I am desperate for control. I would rather hurt myself—metaphorically stab myself—than let anyone else hold the knife. I struggle to come into my body and simply *be*. I do not trust my own body to take the reins. And now someone is asking me, urging me, to let my body release anger. I am doomed to fail.

"I'm just not strong enough," I mutter. I tuck my hair behind my ear and stare at the ground, remembering the asphalt yard of my grade school.

"Sometimes it helps to think of someone you want to punish," she tells me.

I hate that there is anyone I want to punish, but I exhale and close my eyes. I block out thoughts of how stupid I feel, how silly I must appear. *Let go.*

This time the jar flies out of my hand, as if charged with some kind of current. It smacks against the wall and smashes into little pieces. I look back at my therapist, shocked.

"The body knows," she says, reaching for a broom.

She is right, of course. My body knows. Of course physical sensations, just like rage, have purpose. They are signals, indicators, meant to lead us to truths. But I don't listen, for fear of what they might reveal.

* * *

It was a late August afternoon when S and Barbara decided we should go for a bike ride on the beach cruisers we'd purchased a few weeks before. They were both excited by the idea, but I was hesitant. I've never been athletic, preferring to walk leisurely around the track in school when the rest of my peers would run.

I toyed with suggesting we stay at the house to lie around and read, but I knew that I'd just sound lame. I was in my first trimester of pregnancy and all I wanted to do was sleep, but my OB had emphasized the importance of exercise. Besides, the bike rides I'd taken with them always ended up being enjoyable.

I've considered myself uncoordinated for as long as I can remember, even as a child. When my father drove me down the street to a paved parking lot to learn how to ride a bike, I'd managed to keep my balance but had never gained the confidence to master the skill. I couldn't learn to trust my instincts enough to relax and find pleasure in the activity.

The hot air filling our lungs didn't make physical exertion sound any more appealing, but as we rode down the street a surprising breeze broke the humidity.

Barbara led us along the side of the road, her hair streaming behind her. She and S were well-matched travel companions, both always ready to dive into the ocean or go for a late-night swim. I watched how they relaxed without envy: I loved them both and yearned to be more like them, following their example and welcoming their influence. Pedaling along, I dropped my shoulders and took a deep breath, glancing at my hips and thinking of the fetus curled up inside me. That morning I'd read that it was now about the size of a fig. I thought of its heartbeat, wondering if it was aligned with mine.

Up ahead, I saw that Barbara and S had made a left turn into a field. She looked over her shoulder and smiled at me, her teeth crooked and charming. "Short-cut!" she hollered. I nodded as I steered off the road, my bike bumping on the new, uneven terrain.

The field seemed vast. As I pushed on, I felt my bike lose speed in the thick grass. The clouds that had offered coverage for most of our ride parted, the breeze stilled, and I broke into a sweat beneath the hot sun. It beat against my forehead.

I could tell S and Barbara were starting to struggle as well: their postures changed, and they appeared to push their pedals with more focused effort than before. A light-headedness overwhelmed me as my chest tightened. The horizon was dramatic: all blue sky and tall green grass. I worried for a second about the baby—how is his heart rate doing now that I am so out of breath?

S turned toward me, and I couldn't help but think of how gross I must've looked—my face has a tendency to get splotches of red whenever I do anything strenuous. My swollen breasts felt sore beneath my over-sized T-shirt, and I was bloated and dirty. I fought my instinct to stop, feeling a new determination rise up in me. *I am with the people dearest to me on a bike ride on a beautiful day*, I thought. *Don't you dare wuss out.*

I pedaled harder, pushing through the discomfort. My thighs burned. I swallowed a chunk of spit. I saw the road ahead and watched Barbara's body bounce on the seat of her bike as she crossed back onto the asphalt.

They slowed down to wait for me, and I felt a rush of tenderness as I registered the familiar shape of their backs hunched over their handlebars. *It doesn't matter what I look like*, I realized. Blood pulsed up through my thighs and I thought again of the tiny life housed in my body. My closest friend and my husband grinned at me lovingly. Without saying a word, we rode on. My eyes welled with tears. I wanted to cry out: *Thank you! What a joy life can be in this body*.

* * *

As a child, I was terrified of stepping on cracks in the sidewalk, anxious that I might "break my mother's back." I believed that my thoughts had an effect on everything from the role I would get in the school play to what my future would hold or how tall I would grow.

This habit of magical thinking has persisted into adulthood. Some of my superstitions: If I plan a trip, I will be sure to get a job. If I dream of someone, I expect to hear from them soon. If I share good news with anyone before it's official, the fortunate event will not happen. My latest is the belief that if I keep my son's name on my body (on a necklace or a bracelet inscribed with his initials), he will remain healthy.

If there is something, anything, I can do to steer the

outcome of events, then I am less powerless. I am less afraid. This notion is so deeply ingrained that even as I confess this, I worry about the jinx I am placing on my rituals. Will my tricks no longer work now that I have shared them?

I often struggle to delineate what is my gut instinct and what is my hypervigilant, superstitious mind playing tricks on me. Audre Lorde wrote, "As women we have come to distrust that power which rises from our deepest and nonrational knowledge."

A logical part of me knows that events are not affected by supernatural forces dictated by me. Still, I don't want that to be true, at least not entirely. I want to believe in some kind of magic, in some kind of power, even one that is outside of my control.

\* \* \*

No one knows what exactly triggers a woman's body to go into labor. During my pregnancy I learned that despite the confidence of doctors who act as if there is no mystery or magic in our physical lives, this is something for which we have no clear explanation. At one of our final appointments, S asked our OB who decided when it was time: the baby or my body.

"Probably both?" she'd answered vaguely, studying her beeper.

Six days before my due date, nearly midnight on a Sunday in early March, my water broke. Earlier in the day, we'd driven to the Upper West Side for our favorite bagels and whitefish salad as a reward for putting the finishing touches on the nursery (we'd also finally hung paintings that had been leaning against walls for years, as if the baby would be judging our interior design).

On the drive home, I'd asked S if we were ready. "Hell yeah we are," he'd said, squeezing my knee.

"I know it's scary," I hummed later, sitting alone on our red couch, my hands on my belly. "But we'll do it together." I wasn't sure if I was addressing my son or my body. Probably both.

THE RUSH OF warmth between my legs interrupted my sleep, and I sat up straight in the bed. I threw the covers off to reveal a growing wet spot on the sheet. The soft light of the TV cast a shadow on my belly, making it look like a crescent moon.

"It's happening," I exclaimed, leaping up.

As S scrambled to get everything ready to leave for the hospital, I labored on all fours, staring at the checkered tile of our bathroom. My body felt like it was cracking open; the pain was all-encompassing, rippling through my core and spreading to every corner of my being. The contractions were coming without a break, and as one peaked, I felt gripped by sudden panic. I was desperate to make the pain stop, but I was trapped. I bit down, clenching my teeth.

"There is no going back," I said to myself, resting

my forehead against the cold floor and lacing my hands behind my neck. I tried to remember to breathe. What would happen now to me and my baby? Our lives were on the line, but there was nothing I could do to ensure our safety. Our survival now depended on the mysterious mechanisms of my body.

Someone had told me that in order to dilate, a woman's brain waves have to slow down and reach a similar state to orgasm. It was odd to think about sex at the moment of childbirth, but as another contraction seared down my spine, it was a relief to remember that my body was capable of pleasure and release. I tried to fill my mind with blankness. I let the contraction consume me.

Suddenly a new sensation: trust. My body had gotten me this far, hadn't it? It was resilient. It had sheltered my growing son for nine months and kept his heart beating while his entire, complicated self developed inside me. Now it was opening up, right on schedule. I knew then that I had to let go. Despite my fear, I calmed. I surrendered.

When we arrived at the hospital, I crawled through the lobby and contorted against the elevator wall. At the delivery ward, a woman asked me my name while I crouched down next to a chair, pushing my head against its arm. I was there but not really. I was inside my body, a machine that was tearing along viciously with no regard for anything or anyone. I concentrated, refusing to let my brain interrupt my body's workings from functioning. It knew what to do. I just needed to stay out of the way.

The sun rose an hour before it was time to begin pushing. Pink and orange light filtered through the blinds into the hospital room. Striped shadows splayed across the walls. As I pushed, I asked for a mirror. I wanted to see my body. I wanted to witness its progress.

I threw up in a small plastic container that a nurse held to my mouth. Everything was bright. There was no color—just white light. It was morning, the city was waking up. I thought about the coffee being consumed, the hot showers, the lovers saying their goodbyes from a night spent together. Millions of people went about their rituals as they prepared their bodies for another day of life. Birth is as unremarkable as any of those small events: at all times, there is a woman's body in labor. It is both so extraordinary and so common, the way our bodies take us through our lives.

I felt a stab in my pelvis and through my lower back. The contractions guided the room; their rhythms determined everything. I announced each time when one began to peak and the nurse, doctor, and S rushed to get into position next to me and then, like a tide, receded and dispersed again. I was rewarded with every push: a respite from the pain and then a glimpse of the top of my son's head.

In the mirror positioned above me I no longer recognized my face: it was puffy and red, and the veins at my temple were pronounced and throbbing. My body was swollen and raw and unfamiliar. Everything had transformed. My baby's heartbeat crackled through the monitor.

I heard a voice say something about how it had been too long, that the baby was too big and I was too small. "May have to get the vacuum," the doctor said. *No*, I thought.

"Push!" S said, holding my head in his hands and pressing his forehead to mine. I shut my eyes.

"You get to meet your son soon!" the nurses had said as encouragement. I'd never before understood when people described birth as a meeting, but now I did.

I FELT HIM, his body on my chest, but more acutely his presence in the room.

In a daze, I held him to me. *Of my flesh*, I thought. The mirror was pushed to the side, but I could still see the place from where he emerged. My body.

# ACKNOWLEDGMENTS

A version of the essay "Buying Myself Back" was printed in *New York* magazine. Thank you to David Haskell for taking a leap of faith before anyone else would, and to Marisa Carroll for choosing that particular essay.

I am so grateful to the readers who shared how my story affected them. You made me feel less alone. You gave me hope.

Thank you:

To Amy Einhorn and the entire team at Metropolitan for their fierce commitment to this book.

To my editors, Sara Bershtel and Riva Hocherman, for their concision, thoughtfulness, and patience. I owe so much to your keen eyes and open minds. Thank you for seeing this book as one that belongs at Metropolitan. And to Brian Lax, who kept us organized.

To Nate Muscato. To my nimble and brilliant agent, David Kuhn. I treasure our friendship.

To Amy, for your support throughout the years.

To Lindsay Galin, who is fearless, hardworking, and always honest.

To Pippa and Mary. Thank you for being my early readers. Your insights made all the difference.

To Liz, for teaching me how to listen to my body.

To Sarah, for grabbing my hand and going down this road with me.

To Josh, who took his precious mask off in order to tell me what he made of my work.

To Lena and all the other writers who welcomed me with open arms.

To Stephanie Danler, whom I emailed out of the blue, attaching long and messy drafts of essays with a plea for feedback. I will never be able to express what it meant to read your words: "Yes, you're a writer." Thank you for always being there. Your kindness, thoughtfulness, and generosity gave me the confidence to write this book.

To Kat, for being my family and for always loving me.

To Barbara. You have filled my life with joy.

To my mother and my father, the first storytellers I ever knew.

To my husband, for showing me how transforming love can be.

To Sly, to whom this book is dedicated. While you grew inside of me, I wrote, hoping to become the best version of myself for you.

## ABOUT THE AUTHOR

EMILY RATAJKOWSKI is a model, actor, activist, entrepreneur, and writer. She has starred in David Fincher's *Gone Girl*, among other films. Ratajkowski has also appeared on the covers of multiple magazines and walked the runway for numerous high-fashion brands. Her 2020 essay for *New York* magazine, "Buying Myself Back," was hailed as a landmark and was the magazine's most-read piece of the year. *My Body* is her first book.